Missionary Translators

Exploring the history of missionary translation of Christian texts in East Asia, *Missionary Translators* offers a comparative perspective between the features of East Asian languages and the historical context of the translation. Focusing on the Bible and Christian theological works, it looks at the intersection of linguistics, translation studies and history. This book discusses the real-life challenges faced by missionary translators in producing Christian texts in East Asian languages.

Students, historians, scholars and those interested in the study of East Asian cultures or translation will find this book to be an insightful and invaluable resource.

Jieun Kiaer is Associate Professor of Korean Language and Linguistics at the University of Oxford. Her research interests include the formation of translingual/transcultural words and dynamic lexicons. She is particularly interested in the role of social media in the global lexicon. Kiaer is the series editor for Routledge Studies in East Asian Translation.

Alessandro Bianchi is the manager of the Bodleian Japanese Library and curator of the Bodleian historic collection of Japanese rare books and manuscripts. After receiving his PhD from the University of Cambridge, he worked at the British Library and the Smithsonian's National Museum of Asian Art and taught at Haverford College.

Giulia Falato is Lecturer in Chinese Studies at the University of Oxford. Her main research interest lies in the history of Sino-Western cultural relations, with a particular focus on exchanges in the fields of pedagogy, moral philosophy and lexical innovation. She also works educational theories and practices between the Han and the Tang periods.

Pia Jolliffe is Fellow at Blackfriars Hall at the University of Oxford. She teaches early modern and modern Japanese history. Her research interests include the history of Christianity in Japan, especially children and childhood during the transition from Sengoku to Tokugawa Japan.

Kazue Mino is Assistant Professor at Graduate School of Education, Kyoto University. Her research interest lies on the history of Christianity in Taiwan during Japanese colonial era, with particular focus on the interaction between the missiological works of a Scottish Presbyterian missionary Campbell N. Moody (1865–1940) and the Taiwanese Church autonomy movements in the late 1920s and 1930s.

Kyungmin Yu is Assistant Professor in the Department of Korean Language Education of Jeonju University, Korea. She received research grants from National Research Foundation of Korea in 2012 and 2020. These projects examined the vocabulary and style in the Korean Bible translation. She has published five books that explore the linguistic and translational features of the Korean Bible.

Routledge Studies in East Asian Translation

Series Editors:
Jieun Kiaer, *University of Oxford, UK*
Amy Xiaofan Li, *University College London, UK*

Routledge Studies in East Asian Translation aims to discuss issues and challenges involved in translation between Chinese, Japanese and Korean as well as from these languages into European languages with an eye to comparing the cultures of translation within East Asia and tracking some of their complex interrelationships.

Most translation theories are built on translation between European languages, with only few exceptions. However, this Eurocentric view on language and translation can be seriously limited in explaining the translation of non-European literature and scholarship, especially when it comes to translating languages outside the Indo-European family that have radically different script forms and grammatical categories, and may also be embedded in very different writing traditions and cultures. This series considers possible paradigm shifts in translation theory, arguing that translation theory and practice need to go beyond European languages and encompass a wider range of literature and scholarship.

On Translating Modern Korean Poetry
Jieun Kiaer, Anna Yates-Lu and Mattho Mandersloot

Missionary Translators
Translations of Christian Texts in East Asia
Jieun Kiaer, Alessandro Bianchi, Giulia Falato, Pia Jolliffe, Kazue Mino and Kyungmin Yu

Understanding Korean Film
A Cross-Cultural Perspective
Jieun Kiaer and Loli KIm

For more information about this series, please visit: www.routledge.com/languages/series/RSEAT

Missionary Translators
Translations of Christian Texts in East Asia

Jieun Kiaer, Alessandro Bianchi, Giulia Falato, Pia Jolliffe, Kazue Mino and Kyungmin Yu

LONDON AND NEW YORK

First published 2022
by Routledge
2 Park Square, Milton Park, Abingdon, Oxon OX14 4RN

and by Routledge
605 Third Avenue, New York, NY 10158

Routledge is an imprint of the Taylor & Francis Group, an informa business

© 2022 Jieun Kiaer, Alessandro Bianchi, Giulia Falato, Pia Jolliffe, Kazue Mino and Kyungmin Yu

The right of Jieun Kiaer, Alessandro Bianchi, Giulia Falato, Pia Jolliffe, Kazue Mino and Kyungmin Yu to be identified as authors of this work has been asserted by them in accordance with sections 77 and 78 of the Copyright, Designs and Patents Act 1988.

All rights reserved. No part of this book may be reprinted or reproduced or utilised in any form or by any electronic, mechanical, or other means, now known or hereafter invented, including photocopying and recording, or in any information storage or retrieval system, without permission in writing from the publishers.

Trademark notice: Product or corporate names may be trademarks or registered trademarks, and are used only for identification and explanation without intent to infringe.

British Library Cataloguing-in-Publication Data
A catalogue record for this book is available from the British Library

ISBN: 978-0-367-46972-6 (hbk)
ISBN: 978-1-032-12938-9 (pbk)
ISBN: 978-1-003-03234-2 (ebk)

DOI: 10.4324/9781003032342

Typeset in Times New Roman
by Deanta Global Publishing Services, Chennai, India

Contents

Preface		viii
Acknowledgement		xv
1	Language learning and negotiation: The experience of Jesuit translators in late imperial China GIULIA FALATO	1
2	Jesuit translation practices in sixteenth-century Japan: *Sanctos no gosagueo no uchi nuqigaqi* and Luis de Granada PIA JOLLIFFE AND ALESSANDRO BIANCHI	24
3	The making of the Korean Bible: A case study of James S. Gale's New Testament and Genesis translations JIEUN KIAER AND KYUNGMIN YU	57
4	A translation designed to guide: Campbell N. Moody's *Pėh-ōe-jī or Romanised Minnan Taiwanese New Vernacular Translation of and Commentary on Romans I-VIII* (1908) KAZUE MINO	81
Index		105

Preface

M. Antoni J. Ucerler, S.J.

Translation is a human activity par excellence insofar as we are always in search of meaning, either when speaking to others or within our own internal thought processes, so much so that the Mexican poet and diplomat, Octavio Paz (1914–1998), famously remarked that 'learning to speak is learning to translate.' (Burke and Hsia 2007, 11). This process requires, however, that we build bridges over cultural and linguistic divides that may appear impassable at first glance. At the same time, it presupposes that communication is possible even across that divide. This implicitly acknowledges a universal horizon of meaning that all cultures, peoples and languages share in some way. As Giulia Falato comments in her essay, it begins with the discovery of the 'Other' and the very practical need to conduct 'negotiations' to enable that dialogue.

History shows that this has been particularly true and powerful in the case of religion. Since time immemorial, human beings have attempted not only to communicate their beliefs to others but to persuade them to share those beliefs and adopt their religious rituals. In the case of East Asia, one striking example is the history of *translation* of Buddhism—geographic *and* linguistic—as it made its way from the Indian subcontinent further east to Southeast Asia and to the countries and cultures of the Sinosphere, from China to Korea and Japan in the north to Vietnam in the south. Another example is the history of Christianity in East Asia, the focus of the essays in this volume.

While Christianity reached China as early as the seventh century, during the Tang dynasty, it experienced a particularly important development from the late sixteenth century, when missionaries began to arrive from the West. Among the first European missionaries, the most famous was Francis Xavier (1506–1552), who founded the Japanese mission in 1549 and died a few years thereafter within sight of the Chinese mainland. Just over thirty years later, Michele Ruggieri (1543–1607) and Matteo Ricci (1552–1610), two of Xavier's fellow members of the Society of Jesus, would begin a new chapter in the history of the propagation of Christianity in Japan and China. Alessandro Valignano (1539–1606), the mastermind of the Jesuits missions in Asia from 1579 until his death in Macau in 1606, instructed Ruggieri and Ricci to begin their task by learning Chinese. He also encouraged the Jesuits in Japan to make greater efforts to master Japanese.

The fundamental inspiration behind this new Jesuit policy of 'accommodation' to the cultures of Japan and China was the intuition that these two civilizations represented a new 'primitive Church' (*ecclesia primitiva*), akin to that of Ancient Greece and Rome. Their role model thus became the greatest missionary of all time, Paul of Tarsus. As he debated with Greek philosophers at the Areopagus in Athens, Paul soon realized that in order to communicate this new faith, he needed to be able to *persuade* his audience, and this could only be accomplished by *translating* both the words and their meaning into Greek and Latin.

In their correspondence with Rome, the Jesuit missionaries often noted how they felt that they faced a similar task to that of Paul (Ucerler 2016, 27–48).

In this endeavour, they relied on a "rhetorical" mindset, supported and encouraged by their educational institutions in Europe and the publication of a curriculum of studies or the *Ratio studiorum* for their colleges. They also made use of the most important cultural invention of their day, the Gutenberg printing press, which allowed for the inexpensive and wide dissemination of knowledge. The potential of such technology was not lost on Valignano, who arranged for a press to be acquired and brought to Japan from Portugal on the return journey of the four Japanese youths, whom he had sent to Europe in 1582 together with their Jesuit mentor, Diogo de Mesquita (1551–1614). As soon as the press reached Japan in 1590, the missionaries began to experiment with the production of both Roman and Japanese movable type. The first book they printed was a compendium of the lives of the saints, the *Sanctos no gosagueo no uchi nuqigaqi* サンクトスのご作業の内抜書き, taken from various European medieval and early modern sources. In the essay presented by Pia Jolliffe and Alessandro Bianchi, we have an analysis of this first 'Jesuit Mission Press' imprint of 1591. The authors make many important points, beginning with how the materiality of the production process itself, previous European typographical conventions and the use of both Japanese and Latin (in Romanized script) influenced the translation as well as the printing process.

They also note how the Jesuits sought to employ native Japanese words to express Christian concepts while leaving other Latin or Portuguese words intact (e.g. *ecclesia, martyr, cruz*). This was true even in other works, subsequently printed in Japanese script. There was at times serious hesitation as to whether key words should be rendered phonemically (thus initially unintelligible to their Japanese or Chinese interlocutors), so that they could be then adequately explained and 'paraphrased' with native vocabulary. The worry was that a serious misunderstanding of the religious differences between Christianity on the one hand and Buddhism, Shinto, Daoism and Confucianism on the other might occur. The hesitation to employ the Japanese word for God, '*kami* 神,' for instance, was borne out of previous failures that had caused major misunderstandings. Xavier himself had mistakenly used the Shingon Buddhist term *Dainichi* (大日), from *Dainichi nyorai* 大日如来 or Supreme Buddha of the Cosmos, to indicate the Christian concept of God.

In China, we initially find a more conscious decision to adopt Buddhist terminology, such as in the case of Michele Ruggieri's first Chinese catechism, the *Tianzhu shilu* 天主實錄 (*The True Record of the Lord of Heaven*) printed in 1584—a point of religious reference that would later be rejected by other missionaries. The author refers to himself in the colophon as '*Mingjian* 明堅,' 'the monk from India' '*Tianzhuguo sen*天竺國僧.' In her discussion of these dynamics in China, Falato notes how these linguistic negotiations employed two different translation techniques, the exploitation of pre-existing terminology and phonemic transcriptions, the latter accompanied by clarifying or explanatory glosses. Her analysis of the two different approaches taken by João da Rocha in his catechetical *Primer* of 1619 and Francesco Brancati's *Lessons* of 1661 illustrate this tension and evolution in translation strategies, as the missionaries struggled to convey their meaning as faithfully but also as comprehensibly as possible.

Jolliffe and Bianchi emphasize how Jesuit translations into Japanese were not simply a 'linguistic transposition' in search of an 'equivalent linguistic transfer,' as if dealing with a mechanical operation of simply substituting one word for another. Rather they employed 'interlingual equivalents,' rewording into Japanese and even verbal to non-verbal or 'intersemiotic translation' via sacred imagery included in the publication. In China, Giulio Aleni's famous illustrated life of Christ or *Tianzhu jiangsheng chuxiang jingjie* 天主降生出像經解 (*Explanations on the Incarnation of the Lord of Heaven*), printed in 1637 in Fuzhou and based on Jerónimo Nadal's 1593 edition of his *Illustrations of Gospel Stories* (*Evangelicae historiae imagines*), is perhaps the highest expression of this visual genre.

Both cases illustrate a Catholic emphasis on transmitting the essentials articles of faith and conveying an understanding of that faith by creating a Christian literature that also appealed to the reader's emotions. This helps to account for the types of books that the missionaries chose to translate, well versed as they were in the *devotio moderna* movement in Europe. Thus, they tended to give more weight to the importance of personal devotion over pure *ratiocinatio* or argumentative reasoning. The Council of Trent did not, however, encourage vernacular translations of the Sacred Scriptures—and this had a profound impact on the Jesuit missions in both China and Japan. The English merchant, John Saris (c. 1580–1643), mentions in his correspondence that the Jesuits had printed a translation of the New Testament in Kyoto in 1613. This is uncertain, as no copies are known to be extant. However, abundant excerpts from the Bible were translated into Japanese and included in a variety of devotional or theological publications. The Jesuits in Beijing secured permission from Rome to translate the Bible into Chinese as early as 1615, but no comprehensive translation projects of the entire Bible would be undertaken until the advent of the Protestant missionaries in the nineteenth century.

The Reformation had brought with it an emphasis on *sola scriptura*, namely the primacy of the Bible over tradition and even Church structures. The resulting need for vernacular translations of this key text thus profoundly impacted the strategies adopted by the American, British and Canadian protestant missionaries in China, Korea, and Japan. Their approach was further influenced by both the theologies they espoused and the languages themselves. In Korea, the formation of the first organized Christian community was quite unique. In the eighteenth century, Korean converts who had come into contact with their Christianity through personal encounters in China and by reading Christian books translated into Classical Chinese brought the faith back to their homeland with them. They also returned with many books that they had acquired in Beijing. The reading of Matteo Ricci's *Tianzhu shiyi* 天主實義 (1603) (*The True Meaning of the Lord of Heaven*) in particular stimulated an animated debate among the Korean literati as to whether Ricci's understanding of 'Heaven (*Tian*天),' the 'Lord of Heaven (*Tianzhu*天主)' and the 'Lord on High (*Shangdi*上帝)' enhanced Confucian philosophy or was simply a dangerous heterodox version of it. This would later occupy the thoughts and writings of 'Tasan 茶山' or Jeong Yakyong (1762–1836), arguably the most important philosopher of the Joseon dynasty.

A century later, in 1885, when the first American Presbyterian missionary arrived in Korea, he already had in his possession a translated copy of the Gospel of Mark. A full translation would be completed two years thereafter by the Scottish Presbyterian, John Ross. Soon a debate ensued as to 'which Korean' should be used for the purposes of translation. Should it be in the spoken vernacular, written in the phonetic script invented by King Sejong the Great (1397–1450) in 1443, should it be in Classical Chinese 漢文 (*hanmun*), the language of the court and of the Korean *yangban* literati or could it be in a hybrid form that used both Chinese characters 漢字 (*hanja*) and the native script 한글 (*hangeul*)? The American missionary, John Livingstone Nevius (1829–1893), had insisted on the use of the vernacular or *Joseon-mal* 조선말. Soon, other missionaries, including John Ross (1842–1915), and James S. Gale (1863–1937), began considering which words should be used to render the word for 'God.' Should words used by the Chinese, including the aforementioned 上帝 (Ch. *shangdi*; Kr. *sangje*) and 神 (Ch. *shen*; Kr. *sin*) be preferred, or should more native words, such as *hanunim* or *hananim* become the norm?

These debates and their consequences for the development of Korean Protestant Christianity are lucidly illustrated in the essay in this volume by Jieun Kiaer and Kyungmin Yu. She links these missionary debates with the wider socio-political question of what written forms Koreans thought at the time they should be using to express their language. She notes how there was great resistance to the universal adoption of Hangeul by the literati class, because they feared that it would undermine the educational monopoly they had enjoyed for centuries. In fact, Hangeul only became the 'national script' 國文 (*gukmun*) in 1894. Without a doubt, the Japanese suppression of Hangeul in 1910 would later lend to nationalist sentiment and its re-adoption in Korea after the end of the occupation in 1945. In the end, Gale's translation advocated for a mixed' script of both Hangeul and Hanja with the aim of 'maximising comprehensibility and accessibility.' Gale's efforts, which would later be criticized and rejected by many of his fellow missionaries, is reminiscent of earlier efforts in China and Japan. He wished for his translation not only to be a literal and faithful rendering into Korean of the Word of God but one that would appeal both to the hearts and minds of his readers. He was convinced that allusions to Buddhist and shamanistic terminology could, in fact, be helpful rather than a hindrance. One such key Buddhist term in Chinese characters was the word for 'compassion' (*jabi* 慈悲), which would also be adopted by Pedro Gómez and other Jesuit missionaries in Japan as early as the 1590s when explaining God's mercy (Jp. *jihi*). As Kiaer succinctly summarizes the point in the case of Korea, it was a debate between 'faithfulness and naturalisation'—one that was never completely resolved.

These are all good examples that point to how the cultures, the languages and historical circumstances influenced the process of translation. Another similar debate took place in Taiwan with the Presbyterian Church of England and their missionaries' efforts to produce versions of the Bible in a Romanised Amoy Vernacular or Minnan Taiwanese, known as *Pe'h-ōe-jī* (POJ). In her essay, Kazue Mino offers the reader a discussion of Campbell N. Moody's (1865–1940) *New Vernacular Translation of and Commentary on Romans I-VIII* (1908) and contrasts his approach with that of Thomas Barclay (1849–1935), who produced his own revised translation of the New Testament in 1916. The debate in Taiwan in the late nineteenth century once again revolved around language in the specific political and cultural context of the time. The main questions included which should be the target audience, the semi-literate 'masses' or the erudite 'literati?' And which medium, Mandarin, a local vernacular, such as Minnan Taiwanese, or Classical Chinese '*wen-li*文理' should be adopted?

Kazue Mino states that Moody's translation of *Romans* reflects a desire to educate his readers, and his expositive style intends to explain the words so as to instruct. On the other hand, Barclay believed that his task was to present the text without excessive glosses so that the faithful would not be hindered in forming their own understanding of Scripture. Barclay's more traditional Protestant approach was not, in his view 'due to carelessness or incompetence, but to a sincere effort to give with scrupulous accuracy the exact meaning of the inspired writer.' (Barclay 1916, 208). For Moody, the missionary was a necessary and experienced guide, while for Barclay the translator was seen as someone who should not interfere with the development of a strong and independent Church. Thus, Barclay rejected the idea of adding unnecessary commentary or attempting to address the socio-cultural or historical circumstances of the Taiwanese readers. His stated aim was to place the Taiwanese converts on equal footing with the ancient Greeks and Romans who had first heard the Gospel preached to them two thousand years ago. Moody's more 'interventionist' approach shared a greater affinity with prior Catholic traditions of translation in both China and Japan. As Joliffe and Bianchi have pointed out in the case of Japan, the very word 'translation' (*honyaku* 翻訳) was rendered by the missionaries as the act of 'explaining' (*explicar*). At the same time, in the Moody–Barclay debate we can hear echoes of parallel discussions that took place in Korea around the same time.

In all these efforts, the missionaries were greatly aided by their native assistants, whose knowledge of their own language helped the missionaries in their efforts to bridge the divide between the Christian message and their target audiences. This collaborative effort left an indelible mark on these processes in China, Korea and Japan, both Catholic and Protestant. In Japan, it was lay people, both men and women (e.g. Hibiya Monica, *c.* 1549–*c.* 1577), as well as the Japanese Jesuits, Paulo Yōhō Ken (1508?–1595), Vicente Hōin (*c.* 1538–1609), Hara Martinho (1569–1632), et al. In Korea, there were assistants or *josa* (e.g. Yi Changjik, 1866–1938), and in China the literati, including Xu Guangqi (1562–1633) and Li Zhizao (1565–1630), who all played their role in the production of these translations. In the Ricci–Xu joint Chinese translation of *Euclid's Elements, Books I-VI (Jihe yuanben*幾何原本), published in 1607 in Beijing, there is a clear indication in the *Preface* that Ricci 'orally dictated the text' 口譯 (*kouyi*), while Xu wrote it down or 'received it with his brush' 筆受 (*bishou*).

While they approached the problem of translation from a wide variety of different angles, both the Catholic and Protestant missionaries faced many of the same cultural and linguistic problems. As Peter Burke and Ronnie Po-chia Hsia have succinctly put it, the 'translators [were] serving two masters and attempting to reconcile fidelity to the original with intelligibility to their readers.' (Burke and Hsia 2007, 7). This fascinating volume is an important contribution to the study of the myriad ways in which the missionaries confronted these difficulties, informed not only by their respective theologies but also by the peoples, languages and cultures they encountered in East Asia and to whom they preached the Christian faith. The decision of the authors of the present volume to bring together essays that explore both the Catholic and Protestant traditions, while comparing and contrasting the dynamics of 'cultural translation' in China, Korea and Japan from the sixteenth to the nineteenth centuries reflects an understanding of the 'connected histories' of these missionary enterprises and makes for a fascinating read.

References

Burke, P., and Hsia, R.P. (2007) *Cultural translation in early modern Europe*. Cambridge: Cambridge University Press.

Ucerler, M.A.J. (2016) The Jesuits in East Asia in the early modern age. A new "Areopagus" and the "*Re*-invention" of Christianity. In: T. Banchoff and J. Casanova (eds.) *The Jesuits and globalization. Historical legacies and contemporary challenges.* Washington, DC: Georgetown University Press, 27–48.

Acknowledgement

We are grateful to Professor Antoni J. Ucerler for writing the preface for this book and the National Library of Korea for supporting the workshop.

1 Language learning and negotiation

The experience of Jesuit translators in late imperial China

Giulia Falato

Introduction

The history of translation and interpreting in China is intrinsically entangled with the discovery of the 'Other' and the necessity to conduct mutually beneficial negotiations, whether of a commercial, diplomatic or broader political nature. Despite the prominent role played by language mediators or 'tongue–men (*sheren* 舌人)' (Cheung 2016, 36) in government affairs over the course of seventeen centuries, details of their origin and background are quite sparse in Chinese traditional historiography.[1] One possible reason for this scarcity of information could be found in the condescending attitude that various dynastic rulers and government officials held towards non-Han cultures over time; it was only when the country's involvement with foreign powers increased that decoding their tongues became essential to understanding—and taking advantage of—Western scientific and technical knowledge. It is not surprising that the years following the Opium Wars (1839–1842/1856–1860), which saw the coercive opening of Chinese ports to international trade and a growing presence of Western nationals in the Qing territory, correspond to the heyday for translation activities in China. However, the so-called introduction of Western learning (*xixue dongjian* 西學東漸) did not originate in the nineteenth century. Its roots are much older and date back to the activities of two major non-Chinese groups: the Buddhist sutra translators, who in the second century arrived at the Chinese capital from the Western Regions[2] and launched a ten-century-long translation movement, and the Jesuit missionaries from Europe.[3] The latter were an order of erudite men who made education and language acquisition the main tools to propagate the Gospel. They managed to enter China in 1583 after three failed attempts and established an enterprise lasting more than a century that was based on accommodating Christian teachings to local customs (*accomodatio*) and evangelising via publications in the Chinese language. Although the Jesuits were by no means the first nor the last foreign agent

DOI: 10.4324/9781003032342-1

2 *Language learning and negotiation*

in the history of the Sino-Western relations, their activities and contribution to the dissemination of European knowledge have attracted the interest of scholars of different backgrounds for decades.[4] This is probably due to their frontline role in a number of key historical events, such as the transition between the 'conservative' Ming and the 'foreign' Qing dynasty, of Manchu origin in 1644 and the shift in global powers, which saw the influence of the Portuguese Padroado (Assistancy) in Asia slowly decline over the seventeenth century to be replaced by France and Britain (Cheung 2016, 122). In the space of just over one hundred years, the Jesuits demonstrated an impressive readiness to adapt to these changes: they learned the Manchu language to honour their teaching duties with the Kangxi 康熙 emperor (1654–1722) and coped with new policies issued by the French authorities and an increasing shortage of funding and manpower. The Jesuits did this while attending to their pastoral duties, preserving their positions at the Astronomical Bureau in Beijing, and defending themselves from occasional attacks from inside and outside the court.[5] In the meantime, they never neglected their literary endeavours: from early catechisms and a corpus of scientific publications aimed at engaging the literati, to the Rites Controversy—which revolved around their accommodation policy and the rendering of key religious terms in Chinese[6]—translation was truly a permanent presence in the Jesuit China mission and the main pillar upon which their activities were based. For this reason, while not denying the paramount contribution of missionaries such as the Protestants, Franciscans and Dominicans to the dissemination of Christian doctrine in late-imperial China, this study focuses on the Jesuits' work and approach to translation. It provides a brief overview of the significance of language learning in St Ignatius' order and on how the pioneers of the China mission approached the Chinese language and its acquisition. It then looks at how the linguistic and cultural competence of the missionaries resulted in specific translation choices, while not neglecting the collaborative nature of the translation and the role of local literati in the negotiation of a new vocabulary. Finally, it examines how the use of phonemic loans evolved in two essential catechisms belonging to two very distinct stages of the missionaries' presence in China: João da Rocha's (1566–1623) *Tianzhu shengjiao qimeng* 天主聖教啟蒙 (Primer of the Holy Christian doctrine, 1619) and Francesco Brancati's (1607–1671) *Tianshen hui ke* 天神會課 (Lessons for the Congregation of Angels, 1661). This paper proposes to demonstrate that, while linguistic negotiations often resulted in the exploitation of pre-existing terms to translate concepts of foreign origin, the use of phonemic transcriptions to render religious terms was generally considered the 'safest option' to maintain doctrinal purity and slowly became systematised. Moreover, while the 'question of terms' has always been a key preoccupation of the Jesuits' translation works, the authors' inclinations to prefer phonemic loans to other translation options can also hint at their attitude towards the accommodation policy.

'La più equivoca lingua e lettera che si ritruovi:' Chinese language in the eyes of Western missionaries

Language learning can undoubtedly be considered the 'transversal theme' that connected and drove Jesuit enterprises around the globe (Brockey 2019, 389). Its paramount role in the missionaries' formation, to support their understanding and expounding of theology, was clearly stated in Ignatius de Loyola's (1491–1556) *Constitutiones Societatis Iesu* (Constitutions of the Society of Jesus, 1558), one of the fundamental documents for the regulation and administration of the Society (*Constitutions*, 1996, 150–156).

In the words of António Vieira (1608–1697), St. Ignatius's Society of Jesus acted as a novel Babel Tower, where all languages were 'acquired and purchased at the cost of much study and great labour, and therefore with many and great merits.' (Brockey 2019, 391). Such an endeavour was also well-framed in the context of the main geographical discoveries of the period, enabling St. Ignatius and his confrères to bring their missionary contribution to the newly-discovered worlds in Asia and the Americas. As a matter of fact, both the *Constitutiones* and the Society's official study plan, the *Ratio atque Institutio Studiorum Societatis Iesu* (Method and System of the Studies of the Society of Jesus, 1599) show evidence that young Jesuits were exposed to language learning, particularly to Latin, Greek and Hebrew, during the earliest stages of their literary formation: these were not only aimed at permeating the message of the Holy Scriptures, but also at cultivating outstanding oratorical techniques. Moreover, the ability of engendering specific beliefs in the listener by means of logical persuasion was a more than desirable competency in a prospective missionary; to this end, pupils spent the earliest years of their education honing their linguistic and rhetorical skills on Cicero or Aristotle's writings.[7]

If the acquisition and use of '*línguas estranhas*' were universally considered crucial tools in 'preach[ing] the Gospel, propagat[ing] the Faith and expand[ing] the Church' (Brockey 2019, 390) all around the globe, their importance was even more vital in the case of the China mission. Ever since Alessandro Valignano's (1539–1606) arrival to Macau[8]—an outpost of foreign presence in Ming territory— in September 1578, he immediately understood that in order to 'open the doors that lead to the Gospel, … there was no other possible way than studying the Chinese language and written texts' (D'Elia, 1942, 141). It was this intuition that paved the way for the establishment of the Jesuit mission in the Chinese territory by Michele Ruggieri (1543–1607) and Matteo Ricci (1552–1610) in 1583, which resulted in a renewed presence of foreigners at the court of the Ming emperors and the introduction of European science, philosophy and religion through the publication of around 450 books in Chinese in just over 100 years (Hsia 2007, 39–51).

The unifying value of the written language in China, which had for centuries contributed to develop and maintain a strong cultural identity, particularly among the official elite of the country, is a feature that did not escape the eyes of the earliest foreign travellers. During a brief visit to Canton in 1556, sixteenth-century Dominican friar Gaspar da Cruz (1520–1570) highlighted the cohesive component of the Chinese script and its political significance, providing a depiction that echoed the notion of *koiné* (κοινή) in ancient Greece:

> In China there are many differences in languages, for which reason many don't understand each other's speech, but they understand each other's writing as do likewise the inhabitants of the islands of Japan, who understand the Chinese through their writings, although they have a different language.[9]

Additional features, which pertained to the morphology or the use of characters, were picked up by other European authors during the sixteenth and seventeenth centuries, such as Gonzáles de Mendoza (1545–1618) and Francis Bacon (1561–1626), who correctly understood and emphasised the intrinsic entanglement between mastering the script and having access to communication, a privilege that was generally limited to educated officials (De Francis, 1984, 85–88). Exhaustive descriptions of the 'Mandarins' language' or *guanhua* 官話 inexorably appeared in the Jesuits' proto-ethnographic works about China that circulated in Europe, starting from Matteo Ricci's *De Christiana Expeditione apud Sinas* (On the Christian Expedition in China), translated from Italian by Nicolas Trigault (1577–1628) and published in Augsburg in 1615. Undoubtedly, Ricci's account set the trend for all the future *relazioni* from China, contributing to consolidating more or less accurate beliefs associated with late Ming culture and society. He correctly indicated language and written texts as a fundamental part of the government, to such an extent that 'even if philosophers are not kings, it can be said that kings [sic] are ruled by philosophers' (Ricci 2000, 26). The logographic nature of characters, 'similar to hieroglyphics,' along with their semantical ambiguity and tonal variety, made verbal communication and dictation particularly difficult—all aspects that were not lost to Ricci's curious eye. The Jesuit noted that 'since ancient times this nation paid more attention to writing well (*bene scrivere*) than speaking well (*bene parlare*), and all their rhetoric and eloquence are embodied in the composition' (Ricci 2000, 27). Although he explicitly referred to *Cuonhoa*[10] as 'forensic language,' used in embassies and judicial hearings, Ricci restated that characters were the main vehicle of communication among different provinces, and even different countries, such as Japan and Korea (Ricci 2000, 27–28).

As previously noted, these themes seem to be quite recurrent in late Ming Jesuit descriptions of China: in an account written in 1640, a few years before the fall of the Ming dynasty when the Jesuits had consolidated their presence in Beijing and in various other provinces of the empire, Portuguese missionary Alvaro Semedo (1585–1658) provided another insightful analysis of both the written and spoken varieties of the language, describing them as syntactically concise, relatively limited in their vocabulary and semantically ambiguous. Attempting a morphological evaluation, Semedo further explained:

> [Words] are all monosyllabic and indeclinable, both nouns and verbs; their use is so flexible that a verb sometimes acts as a noun and a noun acts as a verb, or even as an adverb, if need be. This makes it easier to learn than the Latin language, on whose grammar we spend all our childhood years.
>
> (Semedo, 1653, 43–44)

After praising the ancient, almost mythical origin of the Chinese script, which is traditionally attributed to the first of the Three Sovereigns or Fu Xi 伏羲, Semedo reintroduced the topic of its influence on the neighbouring countries, where characters were understood even if read in different ways (Semedo 1653, 45). Such an observation was restated and expanded by Jesuit historian Daniello Bartoli (1608–1685) in his *Dell'Istoria della Compagnia de Gesu: La Cina* (On the History of the Society of Jesus: China, 1663):

> Characters also have another unique privilege ... which is that they are understandable also for the other neighbouring countries of China, such as Japan, Korea, Cocincina [i.e. South Vietnam], Tunchin [i.e. Vietnam] and even Siam and Cambodia ... As it happens, these [countries] all have their own languages, which are different and unintelligible among one another (the same goes for certain provinces in China), but nevertheless they all read the script of China and pronounce the same character in a different way, according to their own tongue.
>
> (Bartoli 1843, 126)

6 Language learning and negotiation

As the main vehicle for the circulation of precepts and ideas at cross-provincial and even international levels, pioneers of the Jesuit China mission made the acquisition of the written language their immediate priority and undertook its study on the same textbooks used by late Ming children, such as the *Qianzi wen* 千字文 (Thousand Character Classic) (Brockey 2008, 243). In his fascinating examination of the historical evolution of the Jesuits' educational programme in China, Liam Brockey (2008, 243–285) picks up on two consistent trends of their approach to learning: collaborative effort and interdisciplinarity, to borrow a term from the modern didactic vocabulary.

From Ruggieri's earliest, frustrating attempts to master some basic characters under the guidance of a local teacher who 'helped him struggling through a few schoolbooks' (Brockey 2008, 246) to the composition of Ricci and Ruggieri's first Chinese–Portuguese dictionary as a compass to navigate the complex semantical universe of Chinese script,[11] and from the establishment of St Paul's College of Macau for newcomers' language training to the compilation of a mission-specific *ratio studiorum* under Manuel Dias the Elder (1561–1639) (Brockey 2008, 256–262) the Jesuits were relentless in their efforts to make language learning a more systematised and efficient process.

Nevertheless, such collaborative aspects of formative and missionary activities did not only exist among confrères: the network of educated officials, the so-called literati, provided the Jesuit enterprise with essential support in terms of logistics, protection, financial assistance and linguistic guidance. If we look at the contribution Xu Guangqi 徐光啟 (1562–1633) alone offered to the late Ming mission, we find his name on a few memorials to the Emperor that justified the appointment of Western fathers at the Bureau of Astronomy;[12] we also see him on the front line defending Christianity against accusations of heterodoxy during one of the darkest periods that the early Jesuits in China had to face,[13] and, finally, Xu and his closest disciples were also involved, from the very beginning, in the composition and publication of scientific and religious texts, authored by Ricci and his confrères. Their names appear in highly-resonant works such as *Jihe yuanben* 幾何原本 (Elements of geometry, 1607), *Celiang fayi* 測量法義 (Methods and principles of measurement, 1608) and *Gougu yi* 勾股義 (Principles of *Gougu*, 1608), to name but a few.[14]

It goes without saying that such a highly cultured dialogue between interlocutors from different linguistic backgrounds could not only rely on the mere knowledge of syntactical structures and basic vocabulary. China possessed a long and consolidated philosophical tradition and considered eloquence and erudition two of the key skills to access official careers. European missionaries had therefore to engage their educated counterparts at the same intellectual level, and, in order to do so, they needed to utilise a multidisciplinary, all-encompassing approach to learning. This didn't only imply a simultaneous cultivation of mnemonic and communicative skills during their linguistic training, in a similar fashion to modern language courses, but also required total immersion in the study of the Confucian canon, namely the Four Books and Five Classics (*Sishu wujing* 四書五經), which were an essential component of Chinese education in elite families. By following the same *iter studiorum* of the late Ming literati, the Jesuits successfully acquired a deeper insight into the Confucian (and Neo-Confucian) ethical system, identifying and exploiting a set of shared values, which could be used in their apology of the Christian doctrine, while searching for proof of a monotheistic origin of the Chinese religion. As we shall see in the following analysis, the Confucian canon was also crucial in providing Jesuit authors with reference vocabulary to convey terms and concepts of foreign origin, although these inevitably underwent a process of negotiation and adaptation.

Translation process and strategies

On 22 July 1619, Nicolas Trigault (1577–1628) returned to Macau after a seven-year-long mission in Europe, where he had been sent as a procurator by the Superior Niccolò Longobardo (1559–1654). This enterprise had taken Trigault a long way from China during a particularly challenging time for his confrères, who were all affected to varying degrees by the wave of anti-Christian and anti-Western sentiments and resulting unrest. Nevertheless, his arrival marked the beginning of a new dawn for the China mission. Trigault's quest for funding, manpower and books can certainly be regarded as a success on all fronts: not only did he return with highly qualified recruits who were meant to play an essential role in consolidating the missionaries' reputation at court, particularly during the Ming-Qing transition,[15] but he also brought back some of the finest literary products Europe had to offer. Great were the expectations around this newly arrived library and its scientific or philosophical value: in the annual letter of 1618, Manuel Dias Jr. (1574–1659) described these texts as one of the means to 'regain the ancient freedom' (after the Nanjing incident) (Dias 1618, 241) while in the preface to Giulio Aleni's (1582–1649) *Xixue fan* 西學凡 (Outline of Western learning), Yang Tingyun made explicit reference to the Jesuits' plan to utilise this valuable corpus for their translation project, speaking of 7,000 texts that had arrived by sea and were ready to be translated.[16]

Although Yang's estimate was evidently an overstatement, the European library brought back by Trigault inaugurated a new stage of the Jesuits' literary endeavours, which by the turn of the eighteenth century had resulted in the publication of 120 scientific texts and 330 religious and moral works.[17] It is worth remembering at this point that such literary productions cannot all be defined as 'translations in the modern sense'—these account for roughly 50 of the works, with the aforementioned *Jihe yuanben* being the most well-known. However, the majority of the Jesuits' compositions were in fact synopses, particularly in the case of religious texts, and adaptations, which were based on one or more European sources and relied on a number of paraphrased quotes from Classical and Renaissance authors.[18]

Their *modus traducendi* also differed from the modern, individual approach to translation and can be considered the result of a two-fold cooperation between the missionary and a native speaker.[19] The content was generally 'construed orally' (*kou yi* 口譯) by a Western father and written down in literary Chinese (or 'received with a brush' *bi shou* 筆受) by an educated gentleman. After being co-signed, the draft was then sent for correction and approval to a committee of Jesuit and Chinese censors (Standaert 2001, 693; Xu, 2006, 9). The creation of neologisms or adaptation of pre-existing terms to convey new concepts to the readers were discussed on a case-by-case basis whenever ambiguous or alien notions occurred. Linguistic (and doctrinal) negotiation was therefore an essential part of this process, one in which both knowledge of the original source and competence of the target language carried equal weight.

It should be noted that team translation was not a unique phenomenon in the history of textual transmission in China: the earliest sutra translators also adopted this *modus operandi* and relied on the mnemonic knowledge of a Presiding Translator (*zhu yi* 主譯), who would recite relevant sutras by heart, which were then transmitted into the current language by one or more interpreters (literally word-measurers *duyu* 度語 or word-transmitters *chuanyu* 傳語). As an activity rooted in diplomatic transactions or interactions with barbarian tribes, the status of translation was gradually elevated thanks to the ever-growing work on Buddhist texts, to which we also owe the first cultural translations (Cheung 2006, 8–9). The various agents involved in such a cross-linguistic negotiation didn't possess the same degree of competence in the Chinese language, which affected their lexical or syntactical choices. Early sutra translators such as Zhi Qian 支謙 (222–252 BCE), for instance, relied on a strategy named *geyi* 格義 (matching the meaning), which consisted of borrowing terms from the main Chinese thinkers (Confucius, Laozi, Zhuangzi) to render key Buddhist concepts. While they proved effective in the early introduction of foreign notions into a new cultural system, this practice soon revealed its inadequacy in elucidating doctrinal differences and was soon replaced by other translation strategies, such as transliterations from Sanskrit or clarifications of relevant terminology (Cheung 2006, 97–98).

Over 1,000 years later, late Ming Jesuit translators were confronted with similar issues and resolved to either adapt pre-existing terminology to their communicative intent or to create a new appropriate vocabulary. There were a number of factors influencing their use of phonemic loans, semantic loans, loan translations and neologisms[20] to explain alien concepts to the Chinese readership, beginning with the missionary's degree of competence of the Chinese language and culture. The earliest stages of the Jesuits' missionary and literary activities in China were characterised by a more 'spontaneous,' almost experimental, approach to translation. Phonemic loans, based on the pronunciation of the main languages spoken within the Society (Latin, Portuguese, Italian) seemed to be the preferred choice in the earliest religious texts, such as Ricci's *Tianzhu jiaoyao* 天主教要 (Compendium on the Christian doctrine, 1605), which introduced terms like *Egelexiya* 厄格勒西亞 from the Latin *ecclesia* (church), or *saze'erduode* 撒則耳鐸德 from the Italian *sacerdote* (priest) (D'Elia 1942, 335; Masini 1997, 539). Due to their polysyllabic structure, significantly different from mostly monosyllabic Chinese words, such terms were evidently unintelligible for the average readership, who were unfamiliar with the language of origin, and were therefore usually clarified and later replaced by loan translations (Masini 1997, 539). If we take a step back to the 1580s, we notice that phonemic loans and loan translations belong to a more 'mature' phase of the Jesuits' exposition to the Chinese language. In the invaluable *Dicionário Português-Chinês*, composed by the pioneers of the China mission (Ricci and Ruggieri) between 1583 and 1588, and discovered only in 1934 by Jesuit scholar Pasquale D'Elia (1890–1963), phonemic transcriptions of religious terms are completely absent, while instead an attempt of *geyi* appears evident. *Igresia* (Church) was rendered as *si* 寺(temple) (Ruggieri and Ricci 2001, 108), Anima (soul) as *xin* 心 (heart/mind) (Ruggieri and Ricci 2001, 42) rather than *ling* 靈, which will be used in later publications and Mandamento (commandment)' as *fadu* 法度 (law, moral standard) (Ruggieri and Ricci 2001, 116) instead of *jie* 誡, and there is no entry for *padre* nor *sacerdote*. This might be a demonstration of the 'blurry understanding' of the Chinese vocabulary that the Jesuits still had at the time or a testament to the fact that they were still experimenting with their translation methodology (Ruggieri and Ricci 2001, 21). Such particular terms also hint at a semantical overlap with the Buddhist (*si*) or Confucian (*xin, fadu*) doctrines, suggesting that Jesuit translators, like their Buddhist predecessors, had to rely on a predetermined canonical vocabulary before developing independent solutions.

The composition of phonemic loans followed specific phonological rules, namely those of the Nanjing variant of *guanhua*. As we have seen, its widespread use was confirmed by the recurring references in Jesuits' accounts on China, while its phonological system was unravelled in publications such as the *Dicionário* and Trigault's *Xiru ermu zi* 西儒耳目資 (Aid to the eyes and ears of Western scholars, 1626). The latter is actually a monumental work, written for the benefit of both the European missionaries and the Chinese literati, as it offered a two-fold analysis (and relevant tables) of the spoken variant of *guanhua* and of the romanisation system. Trigault's publication acted as a standard dictionary for the China mission and has continued offering an invaluable reference for Latin-Chinese and Chinese-Latin transcriptions, even in modern religious works.[21] Despite these praiseworthy attempts to codify the phonology of the local language, the production of phonemic loans reveals some differences in the selection of characters to indicate specific sounds. The most notable example is perhaps the transcription of the Latin term *philosophia* as it appears in Alfonso Vagnone's (1568–1640) *Xixue* 西學 (Western learning, c. 1615, published in 1632) and Giulio Aleni's *Xixue fan* 西學凡 (Outline of the Western learning, 1623). The two phonemic loans, *feiluosuofeiya* 費羅所非亞 (Vagnone) and *feilusuofeiya* 斐祿所非亞 (Aleni), differed in particular in the use of the morphemes *fei* 費/斐, *luo* 羅/*lu* 祿, which were possibly influenced by the *xiangtan* 鄉談 (local dialect) of their area. Studies on the *Dicionário* showed that the standard pronunciation of *fei* 費 was actually *fi*, which might explain its use by the then Superior of the Nanjing residence, Vagnone (Ruggieri and Ricci 2001, 114).

It appears that phonemic loans were the primary choice authors employed when first introducing concepts directly related to European culture, which didn't possess a lexical equivalent in Chinese. The phonemic transcription of the term *philosophia*, as we have seen, mostly appeared in late Ming publications that dealt with this particular branch of Western education (Falato 2020, 121),[22] but it had its limitations: in order to exploit its full semantical potential and to make the term immediately understandable by the readership, Jesuit authors had once again to rely on the canonical literature. Hence, *feiluosuofeiya* was explained by Vagnone as the discipline which 'interprets the study of the investigation of things and fathoming of principles (*gewu qiongli* 格物窮理),' (Vagnone 1996, 377) a clear reference to Neo-Confucianism (or *Lixue* 理學), the official doctrine during the Ming and Qing periods. The semantic loans *lixue* 理學 (the study of principle) and *xingxue* 性學 (the study of human nature) along with the loan-translation *like* 理科, created by Aleni (Masini 1997, 550) are but three of the many renderings of the term in late Ming Jesuit publications (Falato 2020, 121). By connecting the European (Aristotelian) philosophy and the Neo-Confucian doctrine, Jesuit authors sought to highlight the universal component of the two traditions, while suggesting that the first could offer fresh tools to benefit the fathoming of principles, one of the core stages of Neo-Confucian education. Such an intention became particularly obvious in Ferdinand Verbiest's (1623–1688) monumental collection of philosophical publications in Chinese, *Qiongli xue* 窮理學 (On the study of the fathoming of principles, 1683), in which *qiongli xue* is interchangeably used to indicate Chinese and European philosophy. By compiling this work and presenting it to the Kangxi Emperor, Verbiest's ambitious aim was to promote European philosophy and particularly the syllogistic method of reasoning ('*litui zhi fa* 理推之法') to provide officials with an 'effective way of thinking' and addressing the most pressing issues of state management.[23] Verbiest's attempt to bridge the gap between the two ways of thinking was, however, not meant to see the light of day, due to the incompatibility between the idea that 'human knowledge and memory are located in the brain' and the nature of '*xin* 心 (heart/mind),' traditionally considered the centre of intellectual and emotional activity (Cheung 2016, 129). Interestingly, despite Verbiest's praiseworthy translation efforts, it was eventually a semantic quibble that prevented Western learning from shaking the foundation of orthodox learning at the Qing court.

Translating key terms and case study

In the previous section we have observed how, in their earliest attempts at navigating the complex Chinese script system, pioneers of Christian and Buddhist translations relied on pre-existing terminology, which at times presented doctrinal ambiguity. If Ruggieri's semantic interpretations in the *Dicionário* and in his first catechism *Tianzhu Shilü* 天主實錄 (True records of the Lord of Heaven, 1584) show the consistent influence of Buddhism, with the author even referring to himself as *seng* 僧 (Buddhist monk) (Ruggieri, n.d., 4–5), as the relationship between the Jesuits and literati became consolidated so did the use of Confucian terminology in missionary publications. We also noted that phonemic loans, usually associated with earliest translation experiments or a lower degree of linguistic and cultural competence, were in fact a consistent occurrence in both late Ming and early Qing texts, but their usage became increasingly contextualised and systematised.

In this section we will attempt a preliminary, comparative examination of two essential catechisms: João da Rocha's *Tianzhu shengjiao qimeng* 天主聖教啟蒙 (Primer of the Holy Christian doctrine, 1619, hereinafter *Primer*)[24] and Francesco Brancati's *Tianshen hui ke* 天神會課 (Lessons for the Congregation of Angels, 1661, hereinafter *Lessons*),[25] highlighting the authors' particular translation strategies and how these should be interpreted in the broader context of the Jesuits' missionary and literary endeavours.

These booklets are similar in format, content and targeted audience but also represent two very distinctive phases of the Jesuit enterprise in China: da Rocha's *Primer* was written during the second stage of the translation project,[26] launched by Longobardo after Ricci's death, and was published in the midst of the anti-Christian wave that saw Nanjing as its epicentre. It is based on Marcos Jorge's (1524–1571) well-known catechism for Portuguese children, *Doctrina Christaã* (Christian Doctrine, 1566 also called *Cartilha*), a text written in dialogue form and translated into at least five different languages for overseas missions, including Japanese.[27] The *Primer* doesn't include a foreword, but it can be speculated that the readership da Rocha had in mind was most likely the commoners of the Jiangnan area, who he sought to evangelise without attracting too much attention from the local authorities. Brancati's *Lessons* was instead the product of a more consolidated stage of the Jesuits' presence in China, when the dissemination of Western knowledge at court was in the hands of a small cohort working at the Bureau of Astronomy while, in the rest of the country, a similarly small group of missionaries looked after a well-established community of Christians and their spiritual education. At this stage, Christianity had already been a part of some communities for a few decades and was being transmitted from 'mother to daughter, from father to son' (Brockey 2008, 346). It had, therefore, reached a more 'familiar' dimension which equally needed to be nurtured, while not neglecting the Jesuits' primary duty of reaching as many souls as possible, attracting more converts.

Essential catechisms possessed all the prerequisites to fulfil such a goal: they provided a straightforward overview of the core ethical norms, ritual and liturgic aspects of Christianity in a plain language, which enabled an even less educated strata of society to achieve a basic understanding of the world view promoted by the Jesuits (Standaert 2001, 598).[28] For this reason, these particular texts were one of the two literary endeavours the missionaries undertook as soon as they set foot on a foreign land, alongside the composition of the so-called *Artes* (grammar or style manuals) (Brockey 2019, 394.). The dialogical form, used by da Rocha and Brancati in their booklets, already had illustrious literary precedents, such as Ruggieri's *Tianzhu shilü* and Ricci's *Tianzhu shiyi* 天主實義 (True meaning of the Lord of Heaven, 1603), and was chosen for its effectiveness in being internalised by the readers.[29] In da Rocha's *Primer*, the two interlocutors are a master (*shi* 師) and a student (*xue* 學), the latter being a personification of the Western missionary in a clever display of deference. Brancati's *Lessons* are instead structured in a question (*wen* 問) and answer (*da* 答) format, evoking an interactive exchange between the intended readership (*tongzi* 童子, namely the young members of the Congregation of Angels) and the Chinese catechists (*sijiao zhe* 司教者), the primary users of the booklet (Brancati n.d., 4).

This format enabled authors to present and explain some of the relevant precepts and prayers (*jing* 經) of the Christian religion to their readers, while providing linguistic or doctrinal clarifications to some of the most controversial aspects. Table 1.1 offers a comparative overview

Table 1.1 Table of contents of da Rocha's Primer (1619) and Brancati's Lessons (1661)

Primer 1619	Lessons 1661
What It Means to be Christian 基利斯當	Rules of the Congregation 天神會規
The Sacred Sign 聖號經(the Sign of the Cross)	Explanation of the Six Essential Principles of the Sacred Doctrine 聖教要理六端解
Paternoster 在天我等父者	Explanation of the Sacred Nature of God 天主聖性解
Hail Mary 亞物瑪利亞	Explanation of the Soul and the Body 靈魂肉身解
Salve Regina 申爾福 or 撒耳物勒日納	Explanation of the Sacred Sign (the Sign of the Cross) 聖號經解
The Twelve Articles of the Creed 聖信十二節	Explanation of the Paternoster 天主經解
The Fourteen Articles of Faith 信德十四條	Explanation of the Hail Mary 聖母經解
Ten Commandments 十誡	Explanation of the Creed 信經解
Rules of the Sacred Church 聖阨格勒西亞定規	Dialogue on the Ten Commandments 天主十誡問答
Seven Capital Sins 罪宗七端	Explanation of the Rules of the Sacred Church 聖教會規解
Seven Sacraments 七撒格辣孟多	Explanation of the Seven Sacraments 聖教七跡解
Theological and Cardinal Virtues 天主三德與四樞德	The Eight True Beatitudes 真福八端

of the contents of the two booklets, which bore many similarities with other catechisms for 'ordinary readers,' such as *Shengjing yuelu* 聖經約錄 (Brief record of the Sacred Scriptures, 1605) and *Jiaoyao jielüe* 教要解略 (Outline of the essential teachings [of Christian doctrine], c. 1615) (King 2009, 168–187).

As can be observed in Table 1.1, key Christian dogmas and norms were included in both texts, such as the explanation of the nature of God, the Creation, the Holy Trinity, Jesus Christ's descent, death and resurrection, the human body and soul, sins, sacraments and, most importantly, how Christians were required to comply with the Ten Commandments. Only the 'Rules of the Congregation' were specifically tailored for Brancati's readership, the members of the Congregation of Angels. While norms, precepts, prayers and other important liturgical aspects generally appear truthful to the original doctrine, an attempt at making Christian teachings culturally relevant can be observed in some sections, particularly in the introduction of the Ten Commandments.

This process appears evident in the explanation of the first commandment, in which da Rocha warned against worshipping 'Buddha, the gods of

Daoism and all demons and idols' (da Rocha n.d., 35; King 2009, 178), while Brancati reminded the reader that venerating evil spirits (*xieshen* 邪神) or following evil practices (*xiefa* 邪法) such as divination (*suanming* 算命), *fengshui* or making offerings to the Stove god (*xian Zao* 獻竈) were all sins against God (Brancati, n.d., 178). When discussing the fifth commandment, 'do not kill,' da Rocha restated that in the eye of God all people are brothers and sisters and therefore they should not harm each other. However, this doesn't apply to capital punishments used in court, which 'don't go against the commandment.'[30] Brancati also picked up on this topic, adding that 'national law doesn't possess selfish intentions (國法無私心),' and therefore killing or beating as punishment for crimes did not constitute a sin (Brancati, n.d., 180). The same tolerance didn't apply to infanticide, a common practice at that time. When families gave birth to many children and could not raise them, they would sometimes end their lives by drowning them. To this, Brancati replied that only God has the power to kill, and He transferred this power to the Emperor (and by extension the officials), and therefore parents who killed their progeny committed a great sin against God.[31] References to the socio-cultural environment are a further confirmation of how accurate the Jesuits' understanding of Chinese rites and practices was and of their diligent work to fit the Christian doctrine into the political hierarchy of the time, in which the emperor appeared as a direct extension of God's power on Earth. At the same time, while the accommodation policy resulted in the Jesuits' conscious efforts to adapt Christian teachings to the Chinese cultural milieu, they clearly did not encourage certain well-rooted 'superstitious' practices, such as the worshipping of local cults and harshly condemned infanticide. This is a topic certainly deserving of more scholarly attention, as it may lead to a different reading of the criticism addressed to the Jesuits at the dawn of the Rites Controversy.

If scientific and philosophical translations had mostly been produced for the consumption of the literati, essential catechisms were the Jesuits' primary tool to spread the Gospel to every societal stratum. Their format and vocabulary, as we have seen, was relatively standardised and is a good indicator of linguistic and doctrinal negotiation evolving over time and across residences. When we look at the terminology used in da Rocha and Brancati's texts, written less than 50 years apart, we notice that some translation choices were consolidated, while in other cases the use of phonemic loans was renegotiated.

The most relevant example of the aforementioned established translations is the term *shijie* 十誡 (Ten Commandments), a semantic loan from Buddhist vocabulary, which appears already in Ruggieri's *Tianzhu shilü* and has been consistently used by Chinese and Jesuit translators in their main religious works.[32] The only exception seems to be Vagnone's *Tongyou jiaoyu* 童幼教育 (On the education of children, c. 1632) where the term was rendered as *shitiaomu* 十條目, due perhaps to the not entirely religious nature of the book (Vagnone 1996, 305).

With regards to phonemic loans, some appear in both da Rocha's and Brancati's catechisms, along with other coeval texts. For instance, the Holy Trinity was rendered as a transcription from Latin (or perhaps Italian) as *Pater* (*badele* 罷德肋), *Filius* (*feilüe* 費略), *Spiritus Sanctus* (*sibiliduo sanduo* 斯彼利多三多).[33] This particular translation had certainly received the official approval of the censors, as it bypassed any doctrinal ambiguity and enjoyed a wide literary fortune.[34] Approved transcriptions from Latin terms were generally the preferred option for liturgical formulae, such as *Ave* (*yawu* 亞物),'*Salve (shen'erfu* 申爾福), *Amen* (*yameng* 亞孟) or relevant doctrinal terms like *Gratia* (*e'lajiya* 額辣濟亞).[35] As previously noted, while sounding truthful to the source language, phonemic loans did not provide the audience with any semantical reference and therefore needed to be clarified, something we can assume happened in both oral and written form. The dialogic format used in many essential catechisms supplied authors with the opportunity to elucidate these and other ambiguous points, as we can see, for instance, in the following excerpt from the *Lessons*:

Q: How to interpret the word 'ave'?
A: 'Ave' derives from the Western pronunciation, it means 'God's blessing.'
Q: And how to understand 'Maria'?
A: 'Maria' is how we call the Holy Mother, it means 'sea star.'[36]

If transcriptions from Latin persist in liturgical translation even in early Qing Jesuit writings, their use to render other doctrinal elements seems to follow a different trend: in da Rocha's *Primer*, terms like Church, soul and 'Sacraments occurred as phonemic loans respectively as '阨格勒西亞 (*ecclesia*), *yanima* 亞尼瑪 (*anima*) and *sagelamengduo* 撒格辣孟多 (*sacramentum*) (da Rocha n.d., 16, 19, 69). This strategy was nothing unheard of and can be traced back to the Jesuits' earliest literary experiments, such as the aforementioned prayer book *Shengjing yuelu* (1605), which is considered the product of Ricci and other missionaries' joint efforts.[37] On the other hand, Brancati's *Lessons* shows a certain reluctance to utilise transcriptions based on foreign pronunciation outside of prayers. By comparing Tables 1.1 and 1.2, it is possible to identify a few semantic loans and loan translations that appeared in lieu of phonemic loans.

What Table 1.2 seems to suggest is a natural, almost predictable shift from the use of semantically meaningless polysyllabic compounds to an attempt

Table 1.2 Selected terms and translation strategies

Primer	Lessons	Meaning
Sheng Egelexiya聖阿格勒西亞	Sheng jiaohui聖教會	Sacred church
Qi Sagelamengduo七撒格辣孟多	Qi ji七跡	Seven sacraments
Yanima 亞尼瑪	Linghun 靈魂	On the soul
Yawu Maliya 亞物瑪利亞	Shengmu jing jie 聖母經解*	Hail Mary

* The latter is obviously the name of a prayer; however, it was included in this table to further validate Brancati's tendency to move away from phonemic loans.

of *geyi*, as in the case of *jiaohui* 教會 (doctrinal gathering, assembly) and *ji* 跡 (sign), both linked to the original connotation of *ecclesia* and *sacramentum* respectively. Such translation choices should therefore be intended as the spontaneous outcome of the missionaries' increasing competence in the Chinese language and culture, or perhaps an effort to make their teachings immediately understandable and relatable to their converts, albeit risking doctrinal ambiguity. Finally, a desire to preserve the Christian roots of religious terminology, or perhaps an attempt at a compromise between dogmatism and accommodation, might be at the basis of da Rocha's rendering of the term *yanima*. By 1619, the notion of soul had already been translated as *hun* 魂 by Ruggieri in 1584 (Ruggieri n.d., 8), and *ling* 靈 by Ricci in 1603 (Ricci 1603, 28) and by Vagnone in 1615,[38] to name but a few, and thus was already circulating as a semantic loan. It is therefore noteworthy that in his *Primer* and in the coeval *Songnian zhugui cheng* 誦念珠規程 (Rules for reciting the rosary c. 1619), da Rocha consistently employed the phonemic loan, while providing a clarifying gloss[39], in a clear attempt to differentiate the semantical nuances of the Western and Chinese terms.[40]

Conclusions

The acquisition of foreign languages had always been encouraged and fostered within the Society of Jesus, as a support to theology and to pave the way for the spreading of the Gospel overseas. For the China Jesuits, mastering the mandarins' parlance was the main tool they possessed to have a voice in late Ming intellectual debate, as demonstrated by the cohesive and transnational value of the Chinese script. However, language competence was only the first step for their missionary endeavours, as it was propaedeutic to understanding the ancient canon of Confucian moral philosophy and to honing the art of composition. 'In China more things get done by using books than by using words,' wrote Matteo Ricci in one of his reports to Rome, while he was composing one of his earliest literary experiments: his treatise on friendship *Jiaoyou lun* 交友論 in 1595.⁴¹ It was thanks to their literary eloquence and stylistic refinement that the seventeenth-century missionaries could embark on an ambitious translation project, which brought Western learning directly to the court of the Ming emperors. The Jesuits' translation endeavours, which became increasingly systematic after Ricci's death, relied on a relatively uniform language learning programme and on a well-established network of educated collaborators who provided financial, logistical and linguistic support to the mission. In order to engage their Chinese counterparts at the same cultural level, early Jesuit authors prioritised the translation of scientific and astronomical books from Europe rather than the Bible, which only began to appear during the eighteenth century, with French painter Louis Antone de Poirot (1735–1813) providing the first adaptation of the New Testament in vernacular Chinese (Cheung 2016, 122).

During their more than one century-long efforts to disseminate Western learning and Christian faith in the East, the question of how to render key religious terms in the target language was a constant preoccupation among Jesuit authors. Like their Buddhist predecessors, they alternated between adapting pre-existing words from the Confucian canon and creating neologisms based on transcriptions from the main languages spoken within the Society. However, both strategies possessed their limits, as they either betrayed the doctrinal purity of the source term or resulted in meaningless compounds that required further clarification, which eventually became one of the core issues of the so-called Rites Controversy. As the most widespread literary works from within the various residences, essential catechisms are useful sources to examine how the question of translation was approached in different periods and by different authors. Our preliminary analysis of da Rocha's *Primer* and Brancati's *Lessons* seems to confirm the general opinion that phonemic loans belonged to the earliest stage of the Jesuits' literary productions, although the transcription of foreign terms later became the preferred option to render specific liturgical formulae, such as those that can be found in prayers. Nevertheless, this paper contends that different translation strategies coexisted at the same time, as in the case of the terms philosophy and soul, suggesting that individual authors had agency in the process of linguistic and doctrinal negotiation and possibly resorted to specific rendering to reflect their personal stand on the accommodation policy.

Notes

1 This study refers to Martha Cheung and Eva Hung's examinations of the discourse of Chinese translation (Cheung 2006 and 2016) and on the role of foreign translators in the Chinese tradition (Hung 1999). Hung's work covers the

period between the second century CE to the nineteenth century, although the first historical records of interpreting activities date back to the ninth century BCE (Hung 1999: 225).

2 In Chinese '*Xiyu* 西域.' This term was used from the Han dynasty (206 BCE–220 CE) to indicate the regions beyond the Yumen guan 玉門關(or Jade Pass), a frontier post on the Silk Road located west of Dunhuang in modern Gansu province.

3 For an overview of the three peaks of foreign translations in China, see Hung 1999, 225–237.

4 There is an extensive bibliography on the subject. Alongside canonical publications like Mungello (1994) and Standaert (2001), the more recent study by Brockey (2008) also offers an insightful analysis of the Jesuits' approach to Chinese language learning.

5 With their influence increasing at court and in local communities, the Jesuits were accused in various instances of attempting to breach the social harmony of the empire and became the target of a series of violent outbreaks, such as the Nanjing Incident in 1616 (see footnote 13). Some clashes also pertained to their positions at the Astronomical Bureau (Cheung, 2016,110), while others involved their views on Chinese rites and translation of key religious terms, which attracted criticism from other orders in China and resulted in the Rites Controversy (see footnote 6) and the suppression of the order in 1773.

6 For a historical overview on the topic and on the specifics of the debate see Standaert (2001: 680–689).

7 For a comprehensive examination of the *Ratio Studiorum* along with its chronological structure and subjects, see Pavur (2005).

8 Valignano was appointed Visitor of missions in the Indies in 1572 and in Macau he founded the Jesuit College of St. Paul.

9 Gaspar da Cruz, *Tratado das coisas da China* (Treatise on China, 1569–1570), quoted from Dinu, (2016, 115).

10 This refers to the *guanhua* variety, as pronounced in the Nanjing dialect.

11 For a comprehensive study of this dictionary and its lexical characteristics in three languages, see Ruggieri and Ricci's *Dicionario* (2001).

12 See, for instance, *Xiugai lifa qing fang yong Tang Ruowang Luo Yagu shu*修改曆法請訪用湯若望羅雅谷疏 (Memorial to respectfully request the appointment of Adam Schall von Bell and Giacomo Rho to the calendar reform, 1630) in Li (2007, 101).

13 This statement refers to the so-called Nanjing Incident, also defined as 'the most terrible persecution that we ever had to suffer' by Jesuit sources, and was launched in 1616 by the then vice Minister of Rites, Shen Que 沈㴶 (1565 – 1624), perhaps as a reaction to the growing influence of the Western fathers on the local community and out of fear that these new religious practices would threaten social harmony. For a first-hand account see Semedo (1653, 256–275). After the first memorial in which Shen accused the 'Western barbarians' of spreading false teachings and of deceiving all the officials who had embraced their foreign religion, Xu Guangqi responded with a heartfelt apology of the Christian doctrine and its values, to show how these could complement the Confucian moral system. See Xu Guangqi, *Bianxue zhangshu* 辨學章疏 (Memorial to explain the doctrine, 1616) in Li (2007, 62–69).

14 For an annotated collection of the main works by Xu Guangqi and the other two 'pillars of Christianity,' Li Zhizao 李之藻 (1565–1630), Yang Tingyun 楊廷筠 (1562–1627), see Li (2007).
15 Among the newcomers who eventually held prominent posts at court or provided a significant contribution to the Jesuits' translation project, some relevant names are Francisco Furtado (1589–1653), Johann Adam Schall von Bell (1592–1666), Johann Terrenz Schreck (1576–1630) and Giacomo Rho (1592–1638).
16 See Aleni (1623, 23). For a study on these publications and how they enriched the Beitang library and other collections in China, see Fang (1948, 1–14).
17 I am referring to Po-chia Hsia's (2007, 39) figures, although Nicolas Standaert's canonical work (2001, 600) actually speaks of 470. With regards to the topical classification of the Jesuit publications, I shall borrow the definition that appears on an anonymous catalogue from 1642: 'Livros que pertencem a explicação da Ley de Deos, e das virtudes e cousas moraes (Books which pertain to the explication of God's Law, virtues and moral precepts)' and 'Livros da filosofia e mathematica (Books on philosophy and mathematics),' which in traditional Jesuit education belonged to the same branch of learning (Bernard 1945, 27).
18 For an exhaustive analysis of the Jesuits' ways of textual transmission see Hsia (2007, 39–42).
19 Such a strategy was not a unique prerogative of the China mission, as can be observed in Bianchi and Jolliffe's study on the Jesuits' translation practices in Japan. See pp. 48–52 of the present volume.
20 I am referring to Federico Masini's definitions, which can be found in his comprehensive examination of how Western translations contributed to the formation of the modern Chinese lexicon (1993 and 1997, 539–555). For what pertains to Buddhist translations, this work refers to the aforementioned *Anthology* edited by Cheung (2006) and to Zürcher's study (2007).
21 For an introduction to *Xiru ermu zi*, see Standaert (2001, 869-870).
22 It should be noted that the term did not disappear at the end of Ming dynasty: it was included, for instance, in an eighteenth-century dictionary of Mandarin language, compiled by Dominican friar Francisco Varo (1627–1687). See South Coblin (2006, vol. 1).
23 For an introduction and translation of the memorial used by Verbiest to present his work to the Emperor, see Cheung (2016,125–129).
24 This study is based on the following digital editions of da Rocha's *Tianzhu shengjiao qimeng* 天主聖教教蒙: BnF, Chinois, 6861–I and BAV, Borgia Cinese, 336.5. Due to the ongoing Covid pandemic, only reprints and online editions of the examined works could be accessed at the time of writing.
25 The earliest edition of this booklet dates back to 1661 and was conceived as a set of moral and practical instructions for the Congregation of Angels, one of the various communities established in Shanghai in the 1640s, which looked after the spiritual education of local children (Brockey 2008, 347). The structure of the *Lessons* was constantly revised in the following editions, with a few addenda and omissions. Due to limited access to primary sources at the time of writing, this study is based on the following digital copies of the BnF: Chinois 6958 (no date of publication) and Chinois 6946, which is a 1739 reprint. The relative fortune of Brancati's booklet, at least in the decades immediately following its publication, is also confirmed by

20 *Language learning and negotiation*

extant translations in Manchu, Korean and Russian languages, see *Tianshen hui ke* 天神會課 in KU Leuven, *Chinese Christian Text Database* (http://heron-net.be/pa_cct/index.php/Detail/objects/9882).

26 The earliest draft of this text possibly dates back to the 1590s with some earlier editions printed before 1619, as suggested by Albert Chan (King 2009, 178). Bernard (1945, 335) also mentions that a booklet with the same title was mistakenly attributed to Giacomo Rho (1593–1638).

27 For a comprehensive examination and usage of Jorge's text, see Abé (2018, 286–307).

28 For an overview and examination of the main essential catechisms composed by the Jesuits at the end of the Ming dynasty, see King (2009, 167–194).

29 To quote Brancati's words in the foreword to his *Lessons*: '然教之而又恐其大理難明，所以著為問答之詞，使之先熟于胸中。 Nevertheless, when teaching [these precepts] one could fear that their great principles are hard to understand, therefore I have written it in the form of dialogue, to enable [the principles] to become immediately internalised (lit. acquainted in one's heart).' See Brancati (n.d., 3).

30 '若朝廷官長用正法刑罰惡人。除民間的害。這等便不爲違誡。 If officials at court use righteous ways to punish evil people, and to eliminate harm among the population, this indeed doesn't constitute a violation of the commandment.' (da Rocha n.d., 40).

31 '殺人之勸，天主但賦與皇帝，而皇帝傳與官府，為父母者，并無殺子女之勸，何可殺之？故父母之殺子女，不論何故，大得罪于天主。 The power (right) to kill is bestowed by God only upon the Emperor, who transfers it to court officials. Parents have no power (right) to kill children, how could they be willing to do so? Hence, the fact that parents kill their offspring, no matter the reason, is always a great sin against God.' (Brancati n.d., 180).

32 I found occurrences of this term in publications by prolific writers like Ricci, Ruggieri, Vagnone, da Rocha and less prolific writers like João Soerio (1566–1606), but also in Xu Guangqi's religious texts such as *Zaowuzhu chuixiang lüe shuo* 造物主垂象略說 (Brief explanation of our Creator's hanging image, c. 1615) or *Shengjiao guijie zhenzan* 聖教規誡箴讚 (Eulogy of the rules and commandments of the Sacred Doctrine, published in 1644). See Li (2007, 321 and 421).

33 Da Rocha (n.d., 6–7). See also Brancati (n.d., 32).

34 An example is Giulio Aleni's *Tianzhu jiansheng chuxiang jingjie* 天主降生出像經解 (Illustrated explanations of the Incarnation of the Lord of Heaven, 1637), a work based on Jerónimo Nadal's (1507–1570) *Evangelicae Historiae Imagines* (1593), where the term appears in the compound *Tianzhu badele* 天主罷德肋 (God Father) (Aleni n.d., 6).

35 The first and last phonemic adaptations can be found in the text of Hail Mary (Ave Maria), while *amen*, as it is known, is the closing formula of every prayer. See, for instance, da Rocha (n.d., 6, 9) and Brancati (n.d., 32, 40, 54). *Salve* refers instead to the prayer Salve Regina (Hail Holy Queen), only included in *Tianzhu shengjiao qimeng* (da Rocha, n.d., 19).

36 '問：亞物兩字，何解？答：亞物是西國之音，謂天主賜福者。問：瑪利亞何解？答：瑪利亞稱聖母聖號，謂海星也。' (Brancati n.d., 55).

37 For an analysis of the text, see King (2009, 172–174). In the excerpt examined by the author, the names of the sacraments are all given as phonemic loans from Latin, the same strategy used by da Rocha in his Primer (da Rocha n.d., 56–62).

38 I am referring to one of Vagnone's earliest literary productions, namely *Xingling shuo* 性靈說 (Discourses on the human nature and soul), written in Nanjing around 1615.
39 At the beginning of the relevant chapter he wrote: '譯言靈魂 (It should be interpreted as 'soul')' (Da Rocha n.d., 66).
40 Da Rocha (n.d., 66–72). See also João da Rocha's *Songnian zhugui cheng* 誦念珠規程, (n.d., 9–11).
41 '... più si fa in Cina coi libri che con le parole' (Mignini 2005, 11).

Cited works

Primary sources (including printed primary sources)

Aleni, G. (1637) *Tianzhu jiansheng chuxiang jingjie* 天主降生出像經解. Jinjiang (Quanzhou): BnF, Chinois 6750.
Aleni, G. (1623) *Xixue fan* 西學凡序. Minzhong (Fuzhou): ARSI, Jap.Sin. II.
Bartoli, D. (1843) *Dell'Istoria della Compagnia de Gesù: La Cina, terza parte dell'Asia*, vol. 1, Ancona: Tipografia G. Aureli.
Brancati, F. (n.d.) *Tianshen hui ke* 天神會課. BnF, Chinois 6958.
Brancati, F. (reprint 1739) *Tianshen hui ke* 天神會課. Beijing: BnF, Chinois 6946.
Da Rocha, J. (n.d.) *Tianzhu shengjiao qimeng* 天主聖教啟蒙. BnF, Chinois, 6861–I.
Da Rocha, J. (n.d.) *Tianzhu shengjiao qimeng* 天主聖教啟蒙. BAV, Borgia Cinese, 336.5.
Da Rocha, J. (n.d.) *Songnian zhugui cheng* 誦念珠規程. BnF, Chinois 7382.
Dias, M. Jr. (1618) *Lettera annua 1618*. Macau: Biblioteca Ajuda, Jesuitas na Asia, vol. 49—V—5, p. 241.
Li, T. (2007) *Xu Guangqi* 徐光啟, *Li Zhizao* 李之澡, *Yang Tingyun* 楊廷筠, *Mingmo Tianzhujiao san zhushi wen jianzhu* 明末天主教三柱石文箋注. Hong Kong: Logos and Pneuma Press.
Mignini, F. (ed.) (2005) *De Amicitia di Matteo Ricci*. Macerata: Quodlibet.
Ricci, M. (1603) *Tianzhu shiyi* 天主實義. ARSI, Jap.Sin I - 44.
Ricci, M. (2000) *Della entrata della Compagnia di Giesù e Christianità nella Cina*. Macerata: Quodilibet.
Ruggieri, M. (n.d.) *Tianzhu Shilü* 天主實錄. ARSI, Jap.Sin I – 189.
Semedo, A. (1653) *Historica Relatione del Gran Regno della Cina*. Rome: Vicale Mascardi.
South Coblin, W. (ed.) (2006) *Glossary of the mandarin language*, by Francisco Varo, vol. 1. Sankt Agustin: W. Monumenta Serica Institute.
Trigault, N. (1626) *Xiru ermu zi* 西儒耳目資. Reprint, Beijing: Beijing daxue 北京大學, 1933.
Vagnone, A. (1996) *Tongyou Jiaoyu er juan* 童幼教育二卷高一志撰 (c. 1632). In: N. Standaert and A. Dudink (eds.) *Chinese christian texts from the Zikawei library*. Taipei: Fujen Catholic University, 239–422.
Witek, J. (ed.) (2001) *Dicionário Portugûes – Chinês, di M. Ruggieri and M. Ricci*. Lisbon: Biblioteca Nacional de Portugal.

Secondary Sources

Abé, T. (2018) Christian catechisms and practice in Japan in the era of the jesuit mission. An intercultural approach. In: A. Flüchter and R. Wirbser (eds.) *Translating catechisms, translating cultures: The expansion of catholicism in early modern world*. Leiden: Brill, 285–307.

Brockey, L. (2008) *Journey to the East: The Jesuit Mission to China, 1579–1724*. Cambridge, MA: Harvard University Press.

Brockey, L. (2019) Comprehending the world: Jesuits, language and translation. *Archivium Historicum Societatis Iesu*, LXXXVIII(176): 389–409.

Cheung, Martha. (2006) *An Anthology of Chinese Discourse on Translation. Volume 1. From the earliest times to the Buddhist Project*. London: Routledge.

Cheung, Martha. (2016) *An Anthology of Chinese Discourse on Translation. Volume 2: From the Late Twelfth Century to 1800*. London: Routledge.

D'Elia, P. (ed.) (1942) *Fonti Ricciane*, edited and commentated by Pasquale D'Elia, S.J., vol. 1. Rome: Reale Accademia d'Italia.

De Francis, J. (1984) *The Chinese language: Facts and fantasy*. Honolulu: University of Hawaii Press.

Dinu, L. (2016) *The Chinese language in European texts: The early period*. London: Palgrave Macmillan.

Falato, G. (2020) *Alfonso Vagnone's Tongyou Jiaoyu 童幼教育 (On the Education of Children, c. 1632). The earliest encounter between Chinese and European pedagogy*. Leiden: Brill.

Fang, H. (1948) *Fang Hao wenlu 方豪文錄*. Beijing: Beijing Shangzhi Bianyi Guanban 北京上智編譯館版.

Henri, B. (1945) Les adaptations chinoises d'ouvrages européens: Bibliographie chronologique depuis la venue des Portugais à Canton jusqu'à la Mission Française de Pékin. *Monumenta Serica*, 10: 1–59.

Hsia, R.P. (2007) The catholic mission and translations in China, 1583–1700. In: P. Burke and R.P. Hsia (eds.) *Cultural translations in early modern Europe*. University Park: Penn State University Press, 39–51.

Hung, E. (1999) The role of the foreign translator in the Chinese translation tradition, 2nd to 19th century. *Target. International Journal of Translations Studies* 11(2): 223–243.

King, G. (2009) The gospel for the ordinary reader: Aspects of six christian texts in Chinese from the late Ming dynasty. *Monumenta Serica*, 57: 167–194.

Masini, F. (1993) *The formation of modern Chinese Lexicon and its evolution toward a national language: The period from 1840 to 1898*. Berkeley: University of California.

Masini, F. (1997) Aleni's contribution to the Chinese language. In: T. Lippiello and R. Malek (eds.) *"Scholar from the west": Giulio Aleni S.J. (1582–1649) and the dialogue between Christianity and China*. Sankt Augustin: Monumenta Serica Institute, 539–555.

Mungello, D.E. (1988) *Curious land: Jesuit accommodation and the origins of sinology*. Honolulu: University of Hawaii Press.

Padberg, J. (ed.) (1996) *The constitutions of the society of Jesus and their complementary norms, a complete English translation of the official Latin texts.* St Louis: The Institute of Jesuit Sources.

Pavur, C. (2005) *The ratio studiorum. The official plan for Jesuit education.* St Louis: The Institute for Jesuit Sources.

Standaert, N. (ed.) (2001) *Handbook of Christianity in China*, vol. 1, 635–1800. Leiden: Brill.

Xu, Z. (2006) *Ming Qing jian Yesuhui shi yizhu tiyao* 明清間耶穌會士譯著提要. Shanghai: Shanghai Shudian Chubanshe 上海書店出版社.

Zürcher, E. (2007) *The Buddhist conquest of China. The spread and adaptation of Buddhism in early medieval China.* Leiden: Brill.

2 Jesuit translation practices in sixteenth-century Japan[1]

Sanctos no gosagueo no uchi nuqigaqi and Luis de Granada

Pia Jolliffe and Alessandro Bianchi

This chapter focuses on *Sanctos no gosagueo no uchi nuqigaqi* ('Extracts from the Acts of the Saints,' henceforth referred to as *Sanctos*), one of the earliest examples of Japanese-language Christian devotional literature. The book offers a collection of hagiographies of saints and martyrs adapted from various sources as well as a partial translation of eleven chapters from the second book of *Introduction del symbolo de la fe* ('Introduction to the Symbol of the Faith') by Luis de Granada (1504–1588), a Dominican friar whose work was widely translated by the Jesuits in East Asia. *Sanctos* was produced in Japan at the Jesuit Mission Press using European movable-type printing technology. The Jesuits imported this printing press to Japan in 1590 with the help of the four young Japanese envoys of the so-called Tenshō-Embassy (1582–1590), the first Japanese embassy to Europe. Significantly, the four young ambassadors also met Luis de Granada after they arrived in Lisbon in 1585, where they presented him with draft translations of his work. They described him as 'a very religious man whom we visited and who is known throughout the world for the holiness of his life, the erudition of his books and the power of his preaching[2]' (de Sande 1590, 168).

Over the decades, *Sanctos* attracted the interest of scholars in a number of fields: historical linguistics, theology, cultural history, literature and bibliography. This study analyses *Sanctos* from an interdisciplinary perspective, treating it as an instance of linguistic and cultural translation. Alessandro Bianchi provides a material and textual examination of *Sanctos*, looking at the structure, production, typographic characteristics and content of the publication (pp. 25–40). Pia Jolliffe approaches *Sanctos* as an example of cultural translation, examining how one chapter from *Introduction del symbolo de la fe* was adapted into Japanese to introduce and explain the concept of martyrdom (pp. 40–51).

This study builds on pre-existing scholarship, such as seminal research on *Sanctos* (Fukushima 1979; Kōso 2006); the Japanese reception of both

DOI: 10.4324/9781003032342-2

Jesuit translation practices in Japan 25

Christianity (Breen and Williams 1996; Miyazaki 2003; Ward 2020) and Christian authors such as Luis de Granada (Orii 2010, 2013; Sobcyzk 2020); accounts of the activities of the Jesuit mission in Japan (Fujikawa 2017; Ucerler 2008), especially those of their publishing endeavours at the Jesuit Mission Press (Satow 1888; Laures 1957; Tenri Tohokan 1973; Tominaga 1978; Triplett 2018); and work on translation practices in Japan (Clements 2015), particularly works dealing with the importance of translating and explaining doctrinal concepts into Japanese (Moran 1992; Kaiser 1996; Farge 2013; Schurhammer 1928; Schwemmer 2014; Sobcyzk 2016 and 2020). For the textual analysis, both authors made use of the following editions: *Sanctos no gosagueo no uchi nuqigaqi*, printed in 1591 at the Jesuit College in Kazusa,[3] and *Segunda parte de la Introduction del symbolo de la fe*, an edition of Luis de Granada's work printed in Zaragoza by Domingo de Portonariis y Ursino in 1583.[4]

An introduction to *Sanctos*: material studies and textual analysis[5]

Sanctos belongs to a larger body of printed publications collectively known as *kirishitanban* キリシタン版 ('Christian editions'), which were produced in Japan by the Jesuit Mission Press in the late sixteenth and early seventeenth century.[6] From a material perspective, *Sanctos* is a complex work, being a Japanese-language book entirely written in Roman script and produced using European printing technology following conventional European typographic standards. Table 2.1 summarises the overall book structure. The book consists of two parts (henceforth identified as ① and ②) bound together in one volume. Each part carries a rich paratextual apparatus: an illustrated title page (Figure 2.2), *errata corrige* and a table

Table 2.1 SANCTOS NO GOSAGVEO NO VCHI NVQIGAQI Bodleian Library, Arch. B f.69 (ex dono John Selden)

PART ① 152 leaves		PART ② 175 leaves	
Title page and engraving	pp. [i]	Title page and engraving	pp. [1]
Text (chapters 1–17)	pp. 1–294	Text (chapters 18–38)	pp. [3]–340
Table of contents	pp. [295]–[296]	Table of contents	pp. [341]–[344]
Errata corrige	pp. [297]–[300]	Errata corrige	pp. [345]–[349]
–	pp. [301]–[302]	–	pp. [350]–[351]
Glossary of relevant Japanese terms with Portuguese equivalents (35 leaves)			

Figure 2.1 Comparison between two historiated initials in Sanctos (bottom) and two others (top) used in books published by Francesco Zannetti.

of contents. In addition, a detailed bilingual glossary of Japanese words (Figure 2.3) is given in the appendix at the end of the volume.

This introduction will explore both the bibliographic and textual aspects of *Sanctos* in order to illuminate the process of adaptation of the original sources into Japanese. The section "The materiality of the language: typography and page layout" will examine *Sanctos* as a physical object (a material texts approach), looking at the elements of design and material production with a view to understanding how the adoption of European typographic conventions and layout influenced the representation of language and some of the linguistic choices in the translation. The section "Content, intertextuality and the concept of translation" focuses on intertextuality (a literary approach), analysing the content of *Sanctos* as an adaptation of pre-existing Christian hagiographic narratives and devotional literature into the Japanese language.

Figure 2.2 Frontispiece of *Sanctos* (part I) with a centrepiece illustration representing an assembly of saints. The text and ornate border were produced using movable-type relief printing. However, the plate mark around the image suggests this was produced using intaglio techniques, such as metal engraving or etching.

The materiality of the language: typography and page layout

Like many other *kirishitanban* published by the Jesuit Mission Press, *Sanctos* displays numerous similarities to European publications and does not conform to the bibliographic standards observed by *wahon* 和本 ('Japanese books') at the time. On the one hand, this is because of its physical format:

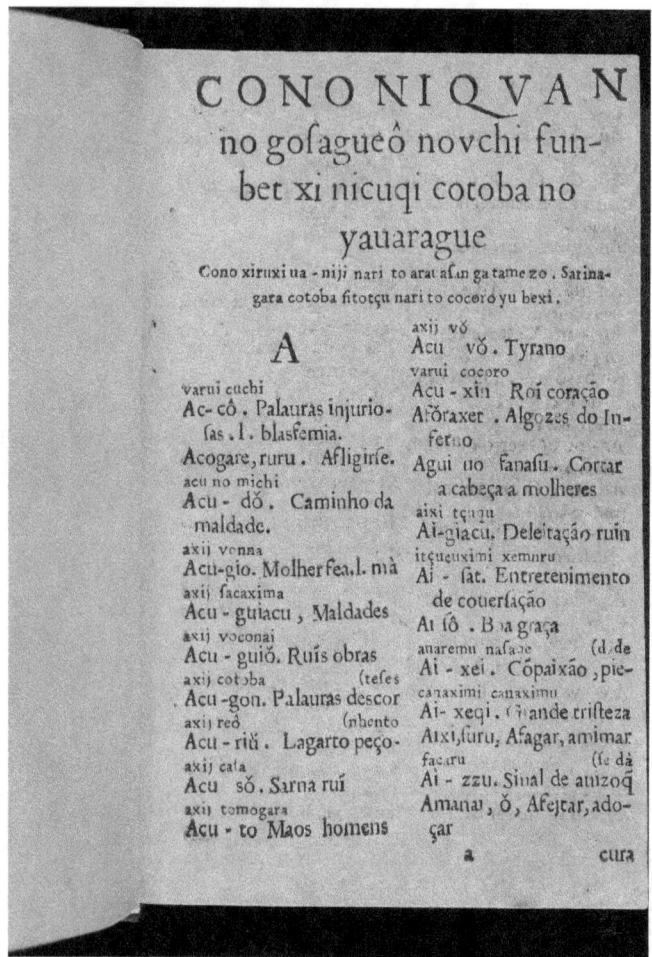

Figure 2.3 First page of the bilingual glossary. Most entries have two translations: e.g. the word *Acu-dō* is followed by an interlingual translation in Portuguese (*Caminho da maldade*) and glossed on top with an intralingual Japanese translation (*acu no michi*), both meaning 'path of evil.' Sometimes intralingual glosses provided explanations using linguistic structures and inversions similar to *kanbun kundoku,* a translation strategy used to make Chinese text accessible to Japanese readers.

gatherings of leaves printed on both sides, then folded, trimmed and sewn together to form a hardbound 8°. On the other hand, this is due to its typographic layout: the way in which the Japanese-language text was displayed and arranged on the page using the Latin script. In this section, I shall study

Jesuit translation practices in Japan   29

the impact that the materiality of language had on the translation by considering (1) the use of the Latin alphabet rather than Japanese scripts, (2) the overall arrangement of the text in horizontal lines and (3) the adoption of European typographic conventions.

One of the most striking features of *Sanctos* and some other *kirishitanban* is the choice to render Japanese text using the Latin script.[7] Rather than using Japanese characters—syllabic *kana* and logographic *kanji*—the Jesuits devised a system of transliteration that allowed them to transcribe the pronunciation of the Japanese text. The choice to use the Latin alphabet was not necessarily determined by technological constraints.[8] In fact, the only extant manuscript of *Sanctos* (Schütte 1940)was also entirely written in Romanised Japanese with a transcription system similar, albeit not identical, to the one used in the printed edition (Fukushima 1979, 350–354). As Higashibaba (2001, 52) suggested, the use of the Latin alphabet was an attempt to make the text more accessible to European missionaries who did not have mastery of the Japanese script.

This choice not only completely transformed the appearance of the written Japanese, but it also determined the overall arrangement of the text in the book. For instance, the shift from *tategaki* 縦書 ('vertical writing') to *yokogaki* 横書 ('horizontal writing') is a direct consequence of adopting a Romanised script instead of *kana* and *kanji*. Until the late nineteenth century, Japanese text was chiefly arranged vertically (Yanaike 2003), with the writing flowing from top to bottom and progressing across the page from right to left. However, the text of *Sanctos* is arranged horizontally, running from left to right and proceeding down each page. This change in orientation not only affected the *mise en page* but ultimately also altered the macrostructure of *Sanctos*. As shown in Table 2.2, the page layout selected to accommodate Romanised text laid out horizontally also determined the adoption of an 'unfamiliar' book structure and pagination, which is typical of European books but is the reverse of what is expected in a *wahon*.

From a stylistic standpoint, the Romanised text of *Sanctos* was rendered using typographical, decorative and orthographic conventions commonly seen in sixteenth-century European printed books. For example, each chapter begins with a historiated initial, 'u' and 'v' were used interchangeably and we even find stylistic ligatures (e.g. ſt, ƈt, Æ, æ) and European notations used to mark contractions, such as the substitution of a '9' superscript for the letters '-us' (e.g. 'De[9]' for 'Deus').

From Tominaga Makita's study of the typographic peculiarities of *kirishitanban*, it is evident that the decorative typeface of these publications was created in emulation of European models. Tominaga (1978, 39–335) also provides an extensive selection of decorative elements used in *kirishitanban* and identifies their sources in European printed

Table 2.2 Comparison between book structure, pagination and text arrangement

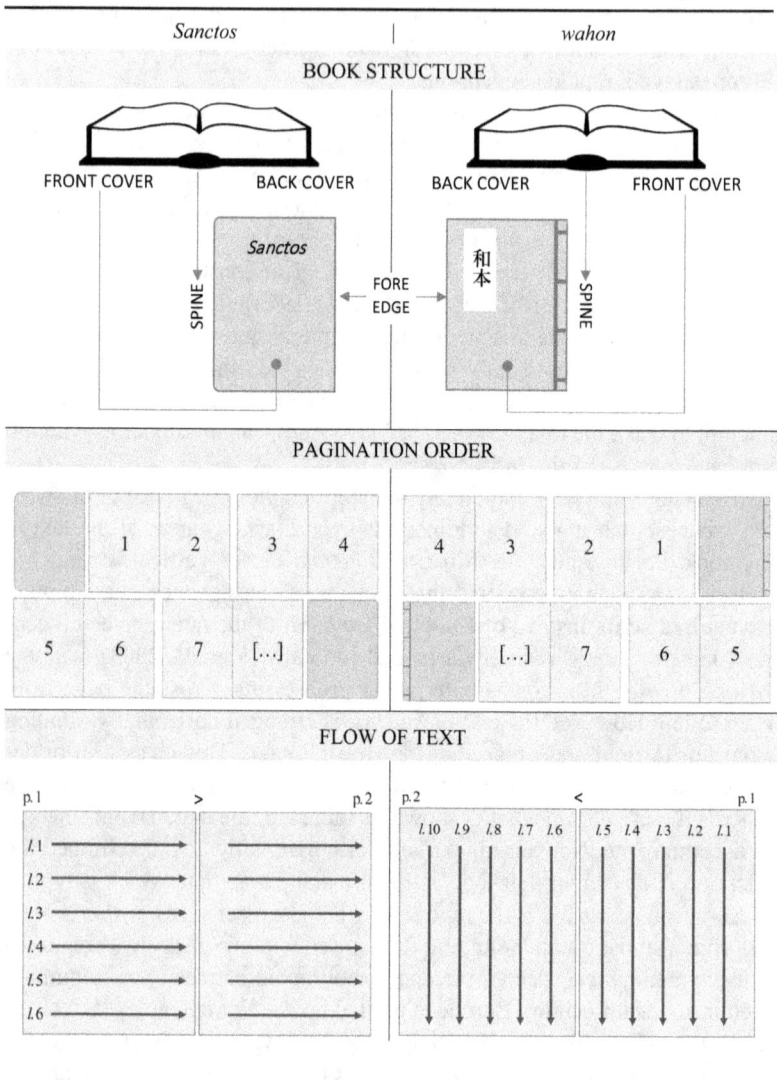

books. For example, Figure 2.1 shows a comparison between two historiated initials in *Sanctos* (bottom) and two others (top) used in books published by Francesco Zannetti, an Italian printer active in Rome in the second half of the sixteenth century.[9]

In addition to these purely stylistic elements, *Sanctos* was printed using an array of functional typographic marks and conventions: line breaks, indentations, spacings, capital letters, punctuation (commas, periods and question marks), pilcrows (¶) and section markers (§). These were likely introduced for two purposes: (1) to enhance legibility, and (2) to organise the text into coherent units (chapters, paragraphs, sentences and words). For example, section markers (§) were paired with Roman numerals to indicate sub-subsections of a longer chapter (e.g. §.I §.II §.III) and were also used to translate Japanese numeric sequences.[10] The use of punctuation marks and word division is yet another interesting case study in this analysis of the materiality of language in *Sanctos*. Premodern Japanese script did not require word spacing, punctuation or any other mark at the end of each sentence. The text resembled a continuous flow of words, with grammatical elements such as verb forms and particles often being the only indicators to mark questions, emphatic utterances or the end of a sentence. In *Sanctos*, however, spacing and punctuation marks are used to separate words and pace the flow of the text. Even more interesting is the use of exclamation and question marks, which sometimes followed grammatical elements such as interrogative particles (*ya* や and *zo* ぞ) or emphatic indicators (*kana* かな and *yo* よ).

- ... fatemo quafŏ tçutanaqi fito cana ! (①23, line 10)
- ... aratani arauare tamŏ cotomo ariqeruyo ! (②130, line 21)
- ... macotoni qidocu narazaru ya ? (②205, line 10)
- ... fafodo made famazamano guiŏtai ni von mi uo yatçufaxe tamai qeru zo ? (②124, line 19)

It can be argued that such punctuation and emphatic markers would have been superfluous for native speakers or those with advanced knowledge of Japanese; the grammar of the sentence would have sufficed. However, European missionaries, especially those with a rudimentary knowledge of Japanese, would have benefited from these functional reading aids. Such aids allowed them to more easily access the content of these texts in private and public contexts, such as personal training and education, communal readings, catechesis or devotional services.

This analysis of the bibliographic aspects of *Sanctos* has demonstrated that the choice to publish the Japanese-language text using the Roman script led naturally to the adoption of a *mise en page* and typographical elements typical of European publications. Furthermore, we have shown that the materiality of language ultimately influenced the overall book structure. In fact, while *kirishitanban* printed in Japanese script display the standard bibliographic format of a *wahon*, titles printed using the Roman script, such as *Sanctos*, resemble instead the format of European publications. The question of whether this could be construed as a form of 'bibliographic translation' (Emmerich 2014) is one that I wish to explore further in future research. However, it is undoubtable that the result of this mix of styles is a complex, almost hybrid object: a Japanese book—produced in Japan and written in the Japanese language—that nonetheless moves away from the bibliographic format that was standard for *wahon* at the time.

Is this all that we can glean from studying the materiality of the language in *Sanctos*? I argue that by engaging with the materiality of this book, we can obtain useful insights into the translation process, especially regarding its morphological and linguistic choices. In fact, the consistent use of Latin script allowed a seemingly seamless integration into the Japanese text of foreign vocabulary and technical terms that lacked direct Japanese equivalents. This provided an efficient solution to deal with the translation of culturally specific words, phrases and concepts that could not easily be rendered from one language into another.

Technical terms pertaining to the Christian doctrine and biblical exegesis are an excellent example (Kaiser 1996), and the attempts made to render the word *Deus* ('God') into Japanese are perhaps some of the most well-researched case studies within the body of Jesuit devotional literature (Kishino 2009). In *kirishitanban*, written in Japanese script, missionaries and their translators adopted various strategies to deal with such terms, including reusing or adapting words in the target language, coining new words or using calques. For example:

- Borrowing of Buddhist vocabulary: *Deus* > *Dainichi* 大日 (the Japanese name of the Buddha Maha Vairocana); *Infierno* > *jigoku* 地獄 ('Hell').
- Creation of nonce words, such as calques of monograms and ligatures used to create logographs: ₫ (*Deus*), ҭ (Jesus), ҳ (Christ), ҳ (Jesus Christ).

Another common strategy was to provide plain transcriptions of these words in syllabic *kana*. Although this approach offered an easy way to circumvent the problem of (mis)translating complex concepts, words often underwent a process of phonetic approximation when transliterated using the syllabic *kana* symbols (e.g. *Deus* > *deusu*; *Gloria* > *gorōria*).

However, in *kirishitanban*, entirely printed using Roman type, foreign words could be transcribed as they would have been written in their original language (Satow 1888, 11). This allowed the integration of any non-Japanese word from the Christian vocabulary into the Japanese text. In *Sanctos* this practice was used for various categories of words including, but not limited to, personal and place names, doctrinal concepts and even entire passages in Latin directly quoted from the Scriptures. Below is an incomplete list of foreign words that were left untranslated:

Sancta Ecclefia	①1	Obediencia	①53	Morte	①203		
Martyr	②2	Epiſtola	①74	Patriarcha	②1		
Euangelio	①5	Bispo	①75	Virtus	②50		
Spiritu Sancti	①15	Philofopho	①79	Rhetorica	②68		
Circuncifan	①17	Apoſtolo	①79	Kyrie eleyfon	②102		
Sacerdote	②21	Babilonia	①149	Emperador	②107		
Sacrificio	①37	Quarefma	①195	Cherubim	②187		
Cruz	①53	Natal	①195	Seraphim	②187		

It is worth noting that the writers of *Sanctos* sometimes applied orthographic modifications to these words in order to reflect changes in grammatical gender and number which were customary in the original language but not required in Japanese. For instance: singular/plural = Apostolo (①79) / Apostolos (①1), Martyr (p. 2) / Martyres (②202); masculine/feminine = Sancto (①170) / Sancta (②190).

Aside from personal and place names or doctrinal concepts, some of these words were common terms that could have easily been replaced with a suitable Japanese equivalent. For example, 'emperor' is sometimes rendered in *Sanctos* using the Japanese term *Micado* (①258) and sometimes as *Emperador* (②107). Similarly, *morte* ('death') is given as the translation for the Japanese word *xi* (*shi* in modern spelling) in the glossary of terms at the end of the book, but there are also times when this word occurs untranslated in the text (e.g. ①203). It is not always clear what drove the writers to leave foreign terms untranslated in *Sanctos* when it came to these ordinary words, but there are times when this choice may be justified by a pragmatic motive. For example, in accounts of the date of a saint's martyrdom in *Sanctos*, the name of the month is left untranslated. For instance, *Auguſt[us]* (②148) was written instead of *hachigatsu* 八月, *Decemb[er]* (②141) instead of *jūnigatsu* 十二月, etc. This is probably because the translators understood the differences between the lunar and solar calendar, where August and December did not correspond to the eighth and twelfth months of the Japanese calendars. Thus, the conscious decision to leave the date 'untranslated' likely reflects an attempt to report accurate information, which in this case was the actual date as expressed in the Gregorian calendar, when the saint is commemorated.

Content, intertextuality and the concept of translation

The second part of my analysis moves away from the materiality of language and the bibliographic characteristics of *Sanctos* to focus more broadly on the literary aspects of the text. It will analyse its content and explore the intertextual nature of the work by looking at the transformations that the primary sources underwent during the translation process.

Sanctos comprises a collection of hagiographies—stories concerning the lives and extraordinary acts of saints and martyrs of the early Roman church—that were abridged and loosely translated into Japanese by the Jesuit missionary community in the late sixteenth century. It is important to stress that *Sanctos* may not have been a direct translation from one single text but rather a patchwork of different stories originally recorded in a miscellaneous body of pre-existing works. The final product was a collage of loose Japanese adaptations, joined together to form a collection of biographies of exemplary figures.

If we are to believe what is stated at the beginning or end of each chapter, *Sanctos* appears to be drawing from a considerable number of primary sources which fall under two main categories: well-known texts and unspecified accounts attributed to influential Christian writers. In the first group, we recognise two books of the Bible (*Genesis* and *Acts of the Apostles*) as well as collections of biographies of saints like *Vitae Sanctorum Patrum* by Saint Hieronymus (ca. 340–420) and *Historia Ecclesiastica*, a Latin translation of Ἐκκλησιαστικὴ ἱστορία by Eusebius of Caesarea (ca. 260/5–339/40). In the second group, there are various references to the writings of exegetes and scholars such as Symeon the Metaphrast and John of Damascus (ca. 675/6–749). Among these, the Dominican father Luis de Granada (1504–1588) occupies a special position: a note to the reader (②169) informs us that the last thirteen chapters (#26–#38) of *Sanctos* are in fact a Japanese adaptation of eleven chapters (#16–#26) from the second book of his *Introduction del symbolo de la fe*.

Judging from the high number of titles and authors directly cited throughout the text (see Table 2.3), *Sanctos* would seem to be an original collation of hagiographic narratives directly translated from these primary sources. In his early survey of *kirishitanban* literature, Satow (1888, 2–6) already provided a full transcription of chapter titles, which also included source texts, arguing that *Sanctos* was 'no translation of a then existing compendium of the Lives of the Saints, but rather a compilation from various sources within reach of the writer or writers.' Although this may seem like a foregone conclusion, such an assessment needs to be nuanced in two ways. Firstly, the information provided in each chapter in *Sanctos* should not be taken at face value. With the exception of Luis de Granada's *Introduction del symbolo de la fe*, it is unclear whether the Japanese missionary community had at their disposal copies of all the books cited in the text at the time *Sanctos* was compiled and printed.[11] Secondly, even if they had access to such sources, there remains the possibility that they were not directly used in the translation process.

We cannot discard the possibility that the writers of *Sanctos* made use of pre-existing anthologies of hagiographic narratives or biographical compendia of saints and martyrs. For example, we know that a book entitled *Cathalagus Sanctorum* is listed among the works present in the early library owned by Jesuit missionaries in Japan (López-Gay 1959, 355). Moreover, Loureiro (2006) suggested that *Sanctos* might have been compiled using a compendium entitled *Flos Sanctorum*, also known as *Legenda Aurea*, which was written by Jacopo da Varazze (1228–1298) in the thirteenth century. This work became incredibly influential, with numerous editions being copied and published in multiple languages over the centuries, until its popularity diminished in the Renaissance (Devonshire et al. 2013, 232–233). Nevertheless, we have evidence that this work was circulating among the Jesuit community in Asia during those years, as the book was translated into Tamil in 1586 (Wicki 1956).[12]

If we assume that *Flos Sancotrum* or another pre-existing compendium of biographies was used to compile *Sanctos*, what, then, is the meaning of the citations consistently recorded throughout the text? It is possible that many of the sources provided were in fact second-hand information. There is evidence of this in Chapter 33. The title heading in *Sanctos* seems to suggest that this chapter was directly adapted from an account 'written by the scholar Eusebius Cesariense' ('Eufebio Cefarienfe toyŭ gacuxŏ caqitamŏ nari,' ②289). Eusebius famously compiled the *Historia Ecclesiatica*, a ponderous work that incidentally seems to have been available to the Jesuits in Japan at the time. However, it is unlikely that Chapter 33 of *Sanctos* was a direct translation from *Historia Ecclesiatica* or any of Eusebius's other works. From the note to the reader (②169), we understand that from Chapter 26 onwards *Sanctos* provides translations of parts of the second book of *Introduction del symbolo de la fe*.[13] However, by comparing the original Spanish text in Luis de Granada's work (see Table 2.4), we realise that the heading of *Sanctos* Chapter 33 is but a summary of the title and opening paragraph in Chapter 21 of *Introduction del symbolo de la fe* (Book II, 124–125). In the incipit, Luis de Granada acknowledges Eusebius's *Historia Ecclesiatica* (Book V) as the source text for his chapter, and the Japanese translators simply incorporated part of that information into *Sanctos*.

The data presented in Table 2.4 is also useful in understanding how the source texts were adapted into Japanese. The underlined parts in the translations of the original Spanish text are the only passages preserved in the Japanese version, while the rest was omitted. Satow (1888, 8–11) and Fukushima (1979, 374–392) already suggested that *Sanctos* did not provide equivalent (i.e. word-for-word) translations of its source text(s). However, this should come as no surprise, as the very title of *Sanctos* clearly states that it is a *nukigaki* 抜き書き, an 'excerpt' in which editors provided a selection of salient passages from longer texts. This process is also openly stated in the original text of *Sanctos*—for instance, the opening

Table 2.3 Conspectus of content and textual sources given in the chapter headings of *Sanctos*

Ch	Content	Textual Source
Section I		
01	St. Peter	Various scholars
02	St. Paul	An account by Symeon the Metaphrast
03	St. Andrew	An account by St. Antonino
04	St. James the Less	An account by Eusebius of Caesarea
05	St. John the Evangelist	An account by the Bishop of Miletus
06	St. Jacob	An account by St. Antonino
07	St. Thomas	An account by St. Isidor
08	St. Philip	Accounts by St. Isidor and St. Antonino
09	St. Bartholomew	An account by Symeon the Metaphrast * noted to be a Latin translation from the Greek
10	St. Matthew	An account by St. Antonino
11	St. Simon and Judas	An account by St. Antonino
12	St. Matthias Apostles	*Not given*
13	St. Ignacio Bishop of Antiochia	Accounts by Eusebius and St. Antonino
14	St. Francis	Accounts by St. Bonaventura and St. Antonino
15	St. Febronia, Virgin Martyr	An account by Symeon the Metaphrast
16	St. Barlaam and St. Josaphat	An account by John of Damascus
17	St. Eustace	Accounts by St. Antonino and Peter Bishop of Anatolia
Section II		
18	Joseph the Patriarch	Book of Genesis
19	St. Sebastian	Section from Book I of a work by St. Antonino
20	St. Catherine	An account by Symeon the Metaphrast
21	St. Alexius	An account by Symeon the Metaphrast
22	St. Eugenia	St. Antonino (Book I) and *Vitae Sanctorum Patrum*
23	St. Steven	*Acts of the Apostles* and *Historia Ecclesiastica*
24	St. Laurence	An account from St Antonino
25	St. Vincent	An account from St Antonino
-	Note to readers (②169) explaining that the following chapters are all taken from Luis de Granada's *Introduction del Símbolo de la Fe*. See the section '*Sanctos* as an example of cultural translation' for a translation of this section.	
26	On the testimony of martyrs	[*Introduction*], Ch. 16
27	On the fourteenth kind of morality	[*Introduction*], Ch. 17
28	Persecution of Diocletian & Maximiliano	[*Introduction*], Ch. 18
29	St. Eulalia's martyr	[*Introduction*], Ch. 19
30	St. Martina's martyrdom	[*Introduction*], Ch. 20; Bishop Adon of Trier

(*Continued*)

Table 2.3 (Continued)

Ch	Content	Textual Source
31	St. Anastasia's martyrdom	[*Introduction*], Ch. 11*; Account by Symeon the Metaphrast
32	St. Clement and Agathangelus's martyrdom	
33	Persecutions under Antonino Vero	[*Introduction*], Ch. 21; Eusebius of Caesarea
34	Persecutions under King Shāpūr of Persia	[*Introduction*], Ch. 22
35	St. Simeon	[*Introduction*], Ch. 23
36	St. Polycarp's martyrdom	[*Introduction*], Ch. 24; *Historia Ecclesiastica* (IV)
37	Account of the battles [won] by the martyrs	[*Introduction*], Ch. 25
38	On the punishment received by the evil kings who persecuted the Christian faith	[*Introduction*], Ch. 26

*These are two subsections of Ch. 20 in *Introduction del symbolo de la fe* (Book II)

of Chapter 32 informs the reader that what follows is in fact an abridgment of an account by Symeon the Metaphrast ('Cono goſagueô uoba Simeon Metaphraſtes to yŭ jennin caci tamŏ mono nari. Ima ſono vchi yori riacuxite yŭbexi,' ②246). In order to accomplish this, the writers of *Sanctos* adopted an array of intertextual techniques defined by Genette (1997, 228–253) as 'quantitative transformations,' i.e., methods of text reduction such as concision, condensation, excision and amputation.

Despite the recurrent use of the word *hon'yaku* 翻訳 ('translation') in the original text, it gradually becomes clear that *Sanctos* is not simply a linguistic transposition. Rather, it was a complex work of translation, which also included direct modifications of the source texts. In examining the meaning of the word *hon'yaku*, Fukushima (1979, 374) suggests that this should be construed according to the Portuguese translation given in the glossary of terms in the appendix of *Sanctos*: *explicar* ('to explain'). This observation resonates with recent scholarship on the cultural history of translation (e.g. Clements 2015; Emmerich 2013), which demonstrated that in premodern and early modern Japan there were a variety of approaches to translation aside from equivalent linguistic transfer.[14]

Sanctos undoubtedly finds its place within this broad landscape of translational practices, which includes rewriting, providing explanations, adding commentaries and making transmedia adaptations, among

Table 2.4 Comparison between passages from Introduction del symbolo de la fe and Sanctos no gosagueo no uchi nuqigaqi

Introduction del symbolo de la fe Ch. 21 (Book II, p. 124-125)	Sanctos Ch. 33 (②289)
DE OTRA PERSECVCION que padeſcio la Igleſia en tiempo del emperador Antonino Vero. Cap. XXI. DEſpues deſta tan grande perfecucion de Diocleciano:añadire aqui vn pedazo de otra que fue en tiempo de Antonino vero, referida por vna deuotiſſima carta de los fieles de Leon de Francia, y Viana (que contiene coſas muy admirables) la qual enxirio Euſebio Ceſarienſe en el quinto libro de la Hiſtoria Ecclcſiaſtica , por eſtas palabras. Nobiliſſimas ciudades de Francia ſon Leon y Viana por donde paſſa el muy caudaloſo Rio Rodano,en las quales en tiempo del Imperio de Antonino Vero acaeſcieró muchas coſas memorables,aſſi por la crueldad delos perſeguidores, como por el fuerte ſufrimiento delos nueſtros. Pero ſera deleytable coſa oyr las recontadas por la carta q̃ los moradores de las miſmas Ciudades eſcriuieron a las Igleſias de Aſia y de Frigia del tenor ſiguiente. §. I. ¶ Losſieruos de Chriſto moradores de Leon y Viana ciudades de Francia a todos los hermanos, que en Aſia y Phrygia tienen la miſma fe y eſperança de gloria, por la Redempcionde Chriſto.	Dai nijû ichi Antonino Vero toyû Roma no teiuo no jidai NI ARIXI ECCLESIANO SAINAN NO coto : core ua França no cuni no vchi Leon to, Viena toyû riôxo no Chriſtan yori caqi tçucauaxitaru jŏ ni arauaretaru uo Euſebio Ceſarienſe toyŭ gacuxŏ caqitamŏ nari. §. I. SAREBA Leon to, Viena no Chriſtan yori Aſia no Chiſtan ye caqi vocurarertaru jŏ ni iuaqu . Icani xitaxiqi qiodai Chriſtan no Redemp çaŏ uo cŏmuri tatematçuru tameni, ſono Gloria no tanomoxiqi uo motçu Fides ichimi no Chriſtan nari. […]

(Continued)

Jesuit translation practices in Japan 39

Table 2.4 (Continued)

Introduction del symbolo de la fe *Ch. 21 (Book II, p. 124-125)*	*Sanctos* *Ch. 33 (②289)*
English Version About another persecution that the Church endured in the time of Emperor Antonino Vero. Chapter 21. After the great persecution of Diocletian: I will add here [information about] another that happened in the time of Antonino Vero, [and it is] referred to by a very devout letter of the faithful [Christians] of Lyons of France and Vianne (which contains very admirable things). This is discussed by Eusebius Cesariense in the fifth book of his *Historia Ecclesiastica*. Lyon and Vianne are the most noble cities of France, where the mighty river Rhône passes. In the time of the Empire of Antonino Vero, many unforgettable things happened, both due to the cruelty of the persecutors, as well as the great suffering of our [brothers and sisters]. But it would be possible to hear those things recounted in the letter written by the inhabitants of these cities to the Churches of Asia and Phrygia. This is what follows. §. I. The servants of Christ, inhabitants of the French cities of Lyon and Vianne, to all the brothers, who in Asia and Phrygia have the same faith and hope of glory, for the Redemption of Christ.	#21* On the calamities [that affected] the Church in the time of the Roman emperor Antonino Vero: this is [an account] written by the scholar Eusebius Cesariense regarding a letter sent by the Christians of Lyon and Vienne in the country called France. §. I. The letter written by the Christians in Lyon and Vianne and sent to the Christians in Asia reads as follows: Dearest brothers, who like us embrace the Christian faith and hope to receive the redemption of Christ** by believing in his Glory. *This number does not indicate the chapter of *Sanctos*, but that of the source text (*Introduction del Símbolo de la Fe*). **The *errata corrige* of part two lists an emendation for page 289 at line 12: Chriſtan > Chriſto. Therefore, the phrase 'Chriſto no Redempçaõ' was used in the English version of this passage.

others. By looking at this publication in its entirety, including appendices and other paratextual elements, we can identify multiple levels of translations, as described in Roman Jakobson's influential study *On Linguistic Aspects of Translation* (1959). For example, the list of difficult terms at the end of the book (Figure 2.3) includes instances of both translation proper from Japanese to Portuguese (i.e., interlingual translation) as well as rewording in Japanese (i.e. intralingual translation). The illustrated title page (Figure 2.2) presents an instance of verbal to non-verbal transfer (i.e., intersemiotic translation). It not only provides a visual representation of the pivotal word *sanctos* but also portrays some of the saints and martyrs described in the text—from left to right in the front row, these are Saint John the Apostle, Saint Christopher, Saint Peter, Saint Paul the Apostle and Saint John the Baptist.[15] Finally, nested within the chapters of *Sanctos* there are also multiple instances of word-for-word translations, such as linguistic transpositions from Latin into Japanese. Often these are direct quotations from the Bible or other liturgical texts, where the quotation is paired with a faithful Japanese rendering of the original text for convenience. For example:

> Sonoyuye ua, Deus reſiſtit ſuperbis, humilibus autem dat gratiam. Eſa. Deus cŏman naru mono uo ſute tamai, fericudaritaru mononi Graça uo ataye tamŏ to yŭ go nari.[16]
>
> This is why '*Deus resistit superbis, humilibus autem dat gratiam*' (Isaiah), which means God casts off the proud but gives grace to the humble. (①153)

The above overview demonstrated that *Sanctos* is indeed a complex and nuanced work of translation, in which multiple layers of bibliographic, syntactic and linguistic permutations coexist within a single work. In addition, *Sanctos* is also a noteworthy example of cultural translation, and the section '*Sanctos* as an example of cultural translation' will explain who the translators were and how translators bridged the gap between cultures to convey complex doctrinal concepts to Japanese readers.

Sanctos as an example of cultural translation[17]

The second part of this chapter concentrates on one of the thirteen *Sanctos* chapters that used Luis de Granada's *Segunda parte de la Introduction del symbolo de la fe* as a source text. It is therefore appropriate to briefly introduce Luis de Granada at this point and to explain why this author became so relevant for the Society of Jesus's missionary translation work in East Asia.

Luis de Granada: a brief introduction

Luis de Granada (1504–1588) was a Spanish Dominican friar. He was born in 1504 in Granada into a poor household. Little is known about his parents except that his father died when Luis was still very young and that his mother had to live from charitable donations she received from a monastery. At the age of ten, Luis began serving as an acolyte in the royal chapel of Saint Francis. He also served in the household of the Count of Tendilla, who provided a humanist education for the young boy. In Tendilla's library, Luis first encountered the works of authors such as Aristotle, Cicero, Virgil and Seneca (Espinosa 2013). He joined the Order of Preachers, the Dominicans, at the age of 19 in 1524 before studying at Colegio de San Gregorio in Valladolid, whereafter he became a very successful preacher and prolific writer. His works were translated into many European languages including Italian, French, German, Latin, Polish and Greek. In post-Reformation England, de Granada's books became bestsellers, appealing to both a Catholic and Protestant readership. Both Catholic and Protestant translators praised de Granada's unrivalled writing skills and compared his spiritual discourses to those of angels (Walsham 2016, 130).

Luis de Granada's fame naturally also reached Portugal, where the then Cardinal (and Prince) Dom Henrique of Portugal (1512–1580) asked the Spanish Dominicans to transfer the famous friar to Portugal. There, Luis de Granada became confessor to the Portuguese royalty before eventually being appointed Provincial of the Dominican Order in Portugal, a role he served from 1555 until 1560. Afterwards, he stayed at the Dominican convent in Lisbon, where he lived until his death in 1588 (Huerga Teruelo 2018). Towards the end of his life, he published *Introduction del symbolo de la fe* (1583) in five volumes. This work became particularly important for Catholic missionaries in Counter-Reformation Europe and overseas missionary territories in Latin America and East Asia.[18] The Jesuits translated the work into Japanese, publishing some parts of it in Japan in 1592.

Why did the Jesuits choose to translate and publish Luis de Granada, a Dominican author? It is perhaps not so surprising that the Jesuits brought Dominican spirituality to Japan and translated it into Japanese for local Christians. Indeed, sixteenth-century Spanish Jesuits studied Saint Thomas of Aquinas at the universities of Salamanca, Alcalá and Valencia, and in this way, the philosophy of Aristotle and the theology of Thomas Aquinas shaped the minds of many Jesuits who went on to become missionaries to Japan (López-Gay 1959, 153–154). The first Jesuit library in Japan—located in Bungo and holding books brought by the Jesuits in 1556—included Thomas's *Summa Theologica* as well as smaller works such as *Summa Contra Gentiles* and *Opuscula Divi Thomae*. The Jesuits did not

Figure 2.4 Portrait of Luis de Granada © Biblioteca del Archivo General de Andalucía. Copia digital: Biblioteca Virtual de Andalucía.

Jesuit translation practices in Japan 43

only bring Dominican books with them to Japan. Importantly, they were also trained to discuss theological matters in the style of Aristotle and Saint Thomas of Aquinas (who was himself influenced by Aristotle). In this way, the Jesuits introduced the spirit and doctrine of Saint Thomas to Japan.

From the above, it becomes clear that de Granada must have been very well known to the Jesuits for at least two reasons. Firstly, during his time in Portugal, he assisted the Jesuits who went to Japan under the patronage of the Portuguese crown. As mentioned above, de Granada was very close to the Portuguese royal family and was thus well known to the Jesuits. Secondly, the Jesuits appreciated de Granada's manuals of devotional literature, which united the thoughts of Saint Thomas of Aquinas with both the Tridentine doctrine and sixteenth-century Spanish spirituality (de Cos, email to the author, 7 August 2020). Next, I will explain how Luis de Granada's *Introduction del symbolo de la fe* was introduced to a Japanese audience.

Cultural translation for a Japanese readership

As mentioned above, *kirishitanban* translations typically tended to omit certain parts of the teachings of the Catholic church. This was likely because certain passages were considered to be too culturally delicate or provocative for a Japanese readership. In addition, translators also occasionally added explanations intended to help Japanese Christians to better understand the teachings of the Church (Schwemmer 2014, 466). It is noteworthy that these omissions and additions were not carried out by Jesuits in Japan without the permission of their superiors overseas; rather, they were only made after receiving approval from the curia in Rome (Orii 2015, 199). Comparing the original Spanish text with the Japanese translation is therefore of cultural interest, as it shows us how Jesuits attempted to introduce Catholic doctrine to the Japanese people in a culturally appropriate way.

In this section, I will compare one chapter of Luis de Granada's original work with the Japanese translation.

As we can see in Table 2.5, although even the chapter number '17' of the Spanish original is translated into Japanese (*Dai 17*), the title of the chapter differs slightly between the Spanish original and the Japanese translation.

In the original Spanish text, the chapter begins with a very long introduction pondering the battle between good and evil. The chapter then introduces the 'martyrs' as soldiers of Christ. De Granada goes on to list the names of some of the male and female martyrs of the early Roman church, such as Saint Laurence, Saint Vincent, Saint Agatha and Saint Eulalia. After this 'general' part, Luis de Granada continues the chapter with a 'particular' section on 'the stories and glorious battles of the holy martyrs'(de Granada

Table 2.5

Introduction del symbolo de la fe Ch. 17 (Book II: 86)	Sanctos no gosagueo no uchi nuqigaqi (②192)
De la décimacuarta Excelencia de la Fe, y Religion Criſtiana, que es hauer ſido confirmada con el teſtimonio de innumberable Martyres. Cap. XVII. English Version About the 14th virtue of the Faith and the Christian Religion, which has been confirmed by the witness of innumerable martyrs. Chapter 17.	Dai 17. Facari gataqi Martyres no cazu vomotte Christian no von voquite no xinjitsu uo arauaxi tamŏ coto: core mata Fides uo tçuyomubeqi 14. ban no tocugui naru coto. 17. To show the truth of the Christian law through the uncountable number of martyrs. This is also the 14th kind of morality [*tokugi* 徳義] to strengthen the Faith.

1583, 90). The martyrs introduced in this section are mostly female virgin martyrs, like the above-mentioned Saint Eulalia who suffered martyrdom as a thirteen-year-old girl in Barcelona. Luis de Granada describes in detail what torments Saint Eulalia and other virgin martyrs had to endure and how—in the case of Saint Barbara—even parents turned against their own children. He emphasises how nothing was able to quench the constancy of 'these weak young women' (de Granada 1583, 91) and quotes from scripture 'the weakness of God is stronger than human strength' (I Corinthians 1. 25). He then writes that one of the greatest mysteries of the Christian faith is that the Passion and death of Jesus Christ are confirmed through the victory of the martyrs, with the martyrs confirming the truth of the holy faith (de Granada 1583, 92). De Granada also emphasises the virtue of 'fortitude,' explaining that it is because of the general admiration for 'fortitude' that people like to read chivalric romance:

> Now I would like to ask all those who read books of false and lying chivalry what moves them to read these books? They will have to answer me that among all the human works that we can see with our physical eyes, the most admirable are those of effort and strength. Because (as Aristotle says) death is the last of all terrible and detested things of all living beings, it causes great admiration among everyone to see a man who despises such a natural fear and is victorious over it. This is the origin of the gathering of people for jousting, bull fights, duels and similar things ... This is also the reason why coats of arms and banners of the nobility are taken from works that symbolize fortitude rather than any other virtue.
>
> (de Granada 1583, 92)

SEGVNDA PARTE
DE LA INTRODVCTION
DEL SYMBOLO DE LA FE, EN
LA QVAL SE TRATA DE LAS EXCE-
lencias de nueſtra ſanctiſsima Fe, y Religion Chriſtiana.

COMPVESTA POR EL MVY REVERENDO PADRE
Maeſtro F. Luys de Granada, de la Orden de Sancto Domingo.

Teſtimonia tua credibilia facta ſunt nimis. Pſalm. 92.

Deus autem ſpei repleat vos omni gaudio, & pace
in credendo.   Rom. 15.

EN ÇARAGOÇA,
En caſa de Domingo de Portonarijs Vrſino, Impreſſor de la
S. C. R. Mageſtad, y del Reyno de Aragon.
M. D. LXXXIII.

Figure 2.5 Segunda parte de la Introduction del symbolo de la fe, Zaragoza: 1583, title page, © Fundación Universitaria Española. Biblioteca.

De Granada then suggests that those who admire the virtue of fortitude should prefer to read the stories of the martyrs rather than made-up chivalric romances. De Granada addresses this contemporary fashion, admonishing his readers that if they truly admire the virtue of fortitude, then they should read about the lives of the martyrs rather than invented stories in chivalric literature.

In comparing the Spanish original with the Japanese translation, I found that, as explained in the section 'An introduction to *Sanctos*: material studies and textual analysis,' the Spanish text has generally been translated faithfully, albeit with some abbreviations and omissions. For example, the above passages on chivalric romances, passages describing the joy of public gatherings for jousting, bull fights and duels and the reference to heraldic symbolism are all excluded from the Japanese version. The simple reason for this omission may be that these were all hobbies and interests strongly linked to sixteenth-century Spanish culture. We know, for instance, that the reading of chivalric romances was also an issue for other Spanish catholic writers. Saint Ignatius of Loyola (1491–1556) and Saint Teresa of Avila (1515–1582) both recount in their autobiographies how as young persons they indulged in reading 'tales of chivalry,' but eventually gave these up for more spiritual readings (Ignatius 1996, 14; Teresa 2002, 13). It is surprising, however, that the translators chose not to translate Luis de Granada's admonishments on chivalric literature and the value of fortitude, as late medieval Japan had its own traditions of epic tales of battles (e.g. *Heike monogatari*) and heraldic symbolism.

There were further cases of omission that were presumably made to render de Granada's text more relevant to the sentiments and mentality of a Japanese readership. For instance, the original Spanish passage on the martyrdom of Saint Barbara explains how her own father locked her up in a tower because of her beauty and how, upon discovering that Saint Barbara had become a Christian, that same father censured her and presented her before judges. The Japanese translation does not include this information about Saint Barbara's father (de Granada 1583, 91), instead beginning with an abbreviated account of the torments she suffered (② 204–205). However, here, the text once again neglects to mention that it was Saint Barbara's own father who eventually decapitated her. Because of her father's role in Saint Barbara's martyrdom, the Spanish text concludes her case by paraphrasing a line from Scripture: 'and fathers will deliver up to death their own children out of hatred for the faith' (Matthew 10:21). This reference to Scripture is likewise excluded from the Japanese text. We may wonder why those who translated this chapter chose to include Saint Barbara's case at all, however, if they were going to omit her own father's role in accusing and eventually executing her. Saint Barbara's father is described in the Spanish text as 'crueller than all beasts' (de Granada 1583, 91). Would this have touched upon Japanese sensibilities more than the sensibilities of a European readership? Surely, Iberian readers were also shocked by her father's behaviour, which is perhaps why de Granada ends Saint Barbara's case by quoting a line from Scripture on how faith can divide children and their parents. Perhaps these issues were considered too radical for Japanese neophytes.

Some names and ages also changed in translation, either by error or deliberately. For example, according to the Spanish text, Saint Eulalia was 13 years old at the moment of her martyrdom (de Granada 1583, 91). A 13-year-old martyr is also mentioned in the Japanese text, although the name of the saint is mistakenly given as Saint Clara (②204). Here, it seems likely that the translator mixed up the names of these two saints: the Japanese names for Saint Eulalia and Saint Clara were *San Orara* and *San Kurara*, respectively—a difference of one character in Japanese. Strictly speaking, it would also have been necessary to translate Saint Eulalia's age, as the premodern Japanese method of counting age differed from European methods at the time. In early modern Japan, children were considered to be one year (*sai*) old at the moment of their birth. They all turned one *sai* older with the start of a new lunar calendar year, even if they were born right at the end of the twelfth lunar month. Accordingly, under the Japanese system, Saint Eulalia's age would have been 14 or even 15 years old.

There are also cases when Spanish sentences are translated in such a way that the Japanese version seems like a clarification of the original text. For example, the sentence:

> Dónde también es mucho de considerar que entre los misterios de nuestra fe, uno de los mayores, que es el de la pasión y muerte de nuestro Salvador, señaladamente se confirma con las victorias de los mártires.
>
> (de Granada 1583, 91–92)

> Here one could ponder a lot that among the mysteries of our faith, one of the main mysteries, namely the Passion and Death of our Saviour, confirms itself in the victory of the martyrs.

is translated into Japanese as:

> Xicaruni Martyres no caxxé ua vó aruji Iesu Christo no go Passion uo vaquimaye guinmi xi tatematçuru tameni, ichidan no temmi nari. (②206)
>
> However, the battles of the martyrs are an even more heavenly taste in order to consider and examine the Passion of our Lord Jesus Christ.

The Japanese sentence simplifies the content of the Spanish sentence, summarising it to state that the martyrs' experiences relate to the Passion of Christ and that the reader should meditate on this mystery. In my view, this example reveals how the translation process may have worked in practice: it seems likely that this passage was translated by someone knowledgeable in Spanish, who was able to explain the general meaning of the Spanish source text for a Japanese audience.

Certain words are omitted (e.g. 'mystery'), while others are replaced with new ones. For example, instead of speaking of the 'victories' (*victorias*) of the martyrs, the Japanese text mentions their 'battles' (合戦 *kassen*). It is curious to read the expression *temmi nari* in this context. The glossary at the end of *Sanctos* translates *tenmi*[19] as *couſa de muito gosto* ('a very tasteful thing') (②404). While it is common in Spanish devotional literature to describe spiritual meditations on the Lord's passion as 'tasteful' or 'delightful,' one may wonder if this may sound strange in Japanese. Regarding this, Orii Yoshimi, an expert on Luis de Granada's reception in Japan notes: 'I don't think it was odd to Japanese readers. Rather I think that it was suitable for translating the concept of spiritual delight or sweetness of Spanish devotional literature' (Orii, email to the author, 13 January 2021). In the next section, we turn to the translators of Luis de Granada's work and the translation processes involved.

Translators and translation processes

Who, then, was responsible for the translation process? The translation of Luis de Granada's *Introduction del symbolo de la fe* into Japanese was likely a long process that spanned several decades. Therefore, it must be seen in relation to the translation practices of the Catholic mission to Japan following the arrival of Francis Xavier in 1549. Initially, the Jesuits were keen to translate everything about Christian doctrine into Japanese. They were advised by Anjirō, the Japanese man who guided Xavier and his companions to Japan, to use Buddhist terms to translate Christian theological terms. For example, as pointed out in the section 'An introduction to *Sanctos*: material studies and textual analysis,' which dealt with translation strategies, the word *Dainichi* was used to translate 'God.' This strategy was ultimately unsuccessful, however, and caused confusion among the Japanese, who thought that another Buddhist sect had arrived from India. In 1555, Father Balthasar Gago suggested a change in terminology, and so the Jesuits started to replace Buddhist terms with Portuguese and Latin terms in their translations. The reform was completed by the end of that year. As the next step, the Jesuits had to revise the catechism developed by Francis Xavier and Anjirō in 1549/50. Father Melchior Nunes, the Provincial, started to draft a new catechism which was completed by Balthasar Gago, who also translated it into Japanese with the Japanese Jesuit Brother Lourenço (Schurhammer 1928, 65). The work, commonly referred to as *Nijugocagio* 二十五ヶ条 ('25 Chapters'), was completed in 1557 or 1558 and went on to be used as a standard work for catechetical instruction throughout the next two decades. There must have been many other informal translations of Jesuit sermons and catechisms. We know, for instance, that in 1561 a 13-year-old boy used his spare time to copy by hand sermons that had already been translated into Japanese. According to Fróis, the boy copied these sermons in order to educate himself and so that he would be able to preach to others (Fróis 2002). In 1562, the Jesuit João Fernandes also used his spare time to translate Catholic books into Japanese. Fróis notes that he did this with the help of 'learned persons so that the translation would be more faithful and pure' (Fróis 2002).

The translators involved in the composition of *Sanctos* were likely a diverse group including European Jesuit priests, Japanese Jesuit brothers and quite likely also Japanese laywoman translators. While many of the translations are anonymous, some parts of *Sanctos* do reference two particular translators at the end of certain chapters: namely, the Japanese Jesuits Brother Yōhō Paulo and his biological son Brother Hōin Vincente. These references would typically read '*Irm. Vicente core ou fonyaku fu*' ('Brother Vincente translated this') (②168). Paulo, Vincente's father, was a medical doctor, and he and his son both joined the Society of Jesus in 1580, where they became known for their excellent translation services. Yet, although only their names are clearly cited as translators, it seems likely that many other people collaborated on the project, which stretched over many years (Koso 206). The Jesuit Gasper Coelho, for example, wrote that at the Jesuit noviciate in Usuki in 1581, various people worked on the Japanese translation of important texts such as the rules of the Society of Jesus; the regulations of the noviciate; the *Contemptus Mundi;* and two or three texts by Luis de Granada (Orii 2010, 68).

Ward (2020), for instance, suggests that in addition to the Jesuit brothers Paulo and Vincente, a Christian Japanese woman called Hibiya Monica was also part of the translation process. Monica's father Hibiya Ryōkei Diogo was known as an important benefactor of the Catholic mission in Sakai. The Hibiya family frequently invited the Jesuits to their home, and it was there—at the Hibiya family home—that the translation of the stories of saints and other texts began. Luis Fróis, for instance, lived with the Hibiya family after the Jesuits had been expelled from Kyoto, where he continued his studies of the Japanese language and translated some of the stories of the saints, likely with the help of the Hibiya family. These initial translations of the stories of the saints into Japanese were first presented orally—in the form of recitations and songs—to local Japanese Christians. This was because some of the Japanese Jesuit brothers were trained *biwa hōshi*: blind itinerant ballad singers who accompanied their tales with the *biwa* instrument. As Jesuit brothers, they used their skill to sing ballads or narrate biblical stories. They would give these performances in private homes, where their audiences typically participated in the performance, thus shaping the ongoing development of these translated stories. This 'writer-singer-audience-response method' was clearly related to the *biwa hōshi*'s practice of orally reciting epic works such as the *Heike monogatari* in social settings, during funerary rites and as part of Buddhist evangelising activities within temples and on public streets. In this way, they 'translated' and disseminated Christian doctrine in a localised manner. Ward suggests that because the stories of women saints in *Sanctos no gosagveo* are extremely sensitive to the nuances of female Japanese speech, it is possible that Hibiya Monica played a role in the translation process (Takao 2019, 189; Ruiz-de-Medina 2003, 124; Ward 2020, 177–178).

It is also possible that students from the Jesuits' schools and colleges contributed to the translation process of Luis de Granada's works. According to the Jesuit scholar López-Gay we can assume that Pedro Ramón, the first Jesuit novice master in Japan, began work on the translation of de Granada's *Introduction del symbolo de la fe* after he arrived in Japan in 1575 (López-Gay 1959, 367). To be sure, translating Luis de Granada's work also occupied the four young Japanese boys who travelled to Rome as protagonists of the Tenshō Embassy in 1582.

Luis Fróis describes how after their arrival in Lisbon, the boys met Luis de Granada himself in the Dominican monastery, presumably on 15 August:

> Returning to Lisbon [from an excursion] they went to see other monasteries where they were very well received and celebrated, especially in Santo Domingo, where they were received by the Prior and Fray Luis de Granada whom they very much wished to see because of his virtue and to whom they showed his books translated into Japanese language and script with which the Saintly Old Man seemed quite pleased.
>
> (Fróis 1942, 36)

Jesuit translation practices in Japan   51

This passage is extremely interesting, as it gives proof of the encounter between Luis de Granada and the boys of the Tenshō embassy. The embassy reached Lisbon in August 1584. At that time, Luis de Granada was almost 80 years old, whereas the boys of the Tenshō embassy were around 16 years old. It must have been a special moment for both parties: for the young ambassadors to meet the famous Dominican theologian and for de Granada to see his own work translated into Japanese script. This detail is particularly relevant for our study on the translation of Luis de Granada into Japanese and suggests that the four young ambassadors carried with them manuscripts of the Japanese translation of Luis de Granada's work written in Japanese script. It was only at a later stage that these translations were printed in Roman characters with the printing press the Tenshō embassy brought to Japan in 1590. The Jesuit scholar Diego Pacheco assumes that these were manuscripts of *Guia de pecadores* or *Libro de la oración y meditación*. Furthermore, he says that the boys must either have brought a completed translation with them from Japan or occupied themselves with the translation during their long journey to Europe (Pacheco 1971, 440). This latter theory is supported by the testimony of the ambassador boys' Jesuit guide, Diogo de Mesquita (1553–1614). De Mesquita mentioned in several letters to Rome how helpful the boys were in translating Catholic texts into Japanese for publication using the printing press. In these letters he highlights the role of Hara Martinho who, after the embassy's return to Japan, became a Jesuit and subsequently translated or helped revise at least three *kirishitan* works: *Guía de pecadores*, the first part of *Introduction del symbolo de la fe* and work on the final revisions of *Imitation of Christ* (Orii 2011, 175; Pacheco 1971, 442). According to contemporary sources, Hara Martinho also had the best Latin ability of the Japanese Jesuits (Moran 1992, 17). The translation of *Sanctos* is therefore best understood as a complex process that involved different groups of people, including both European and Japanese Jesuits as well as Japanese laypeople (both men and women) who worked over a considerable span of time to render a variety of texts into Japanese.

Concluding remarks

In this chapter we explored Jesuit translation practices in sixteenth-century Japan by examining the work *Sanctos no gosagueo no uchi nuqigaqi* and the way that some parts of Luis de Granada's *Introduction del symbolo de la fe* were translated from Spanish, both linguistically and culturally, into the linguistic and socio-cultural context of late sixteenth-century Japan. We introduced *Sanctos* as a *kirishitanban*, i.e., a publication produced by the Jesuit Mission Press to Japan, discussing the materiality of the text and the translation concepts that shaped the way different European source texts were rendered into Japanese. This allowed us to see the complex processes involved in Jesuit translation practices in this period. These processes clearly involved cooperation and collaboration between the Jesuits and their friends and thus included European missionaries, Japanese members of the Society of Jesus and Japanese laypeople. Such cooperation shares similarities with Jesuit printing activities in Counter-Reformation Europe, where many laypeople risked their lives to aid the publication and dissemination of texts printed at Jesuit presses in Elizabethan England.

It is also significant that Luis de Granada was so widely translated into Japanese. By choosing the works of this Dominican friar, the Jesuits brought the spirit of the Counter-Reformation to the overseas missionary territories of the East Indies. Of course, the political-economic and socio-cultural context of late sixteenth-century Japan differed greatly from the European situation. Therefore, translation for a Japanese audience requested not only linguistic skills but also the ability to 'culturally translate' the content of works by Luis de Granada and others so as to render them meaningful to Japanese readers.

Sanctos is an excellent example of sixteenth-century Jesuit translation practices within a transnational context that worked to bring Counter-Reformation Europe and late sixteenth-century Japan closer together. Significantly, this cultural approach to translation centred around the notion of 'martyrdom.' It is an interesting coincidence that many of those who were involved in translating a book about martyrs—or their students and offspring—died as martyrs, just like the majority of the saints in the book.

Notes

1 Both authors are grateful to Giulia Falato and Katja Triplett who commented on early versions of this chapter.
2 Translated from Latin by Pia Jolliffe.
3 More precisely, the Bodleian Library copy (Arch. B f.69) which arrived in Oxford with John Selden's collection in 1659. A digitised version is available online on Digital.Bodleian. Another printed copy is housed in Biblioteca Marciana (Kōso 2006) and a manuscript copy at Bibliotheca Apostolica Vaticana. (Schütte 1940).
4 Specifically, the copy of Fundación Universitaria Española (XIV/529), which is accessible through Biblioteca Digital de Madrid's online portal. This edition was chosen in consideration of the publication year of *Sanctos* (1591) and because it predates the visit to Spain of the Tenshō Embassy in 1584. Although this is a purely speculative hypothesis, this edition might have arrived in Japan before the publication of *Sanctos*.
5 Alessandro Bianchi is grateful to Dr Laura Moretti and Dr Ellis Tinos for the constructive discussions and helpful comments at the early stages of this work.

6 These works bear witness to the prolific activities of Jesuit Missionaries in the Archipelago and, at the same time, are an important milestone in the history of printing and books in Japan. For an overview of missionary printing in Asia see Ucerler (2010).
7 Fukushima (1979, 393–406) provides a thorough description of the transliteration of *Sanctos*.
8 The earliest extant publication written entirely in Japanese scripts is the dictionary *Rakuyōshū* 落葉集 (1598), but scholars suggested that other undated works and fragments written in *kana* and *kanji* may have been printed around the time *Sanctos* was produced (Tenri Tohokan 1973, 160; Tominaga 1978, 27–28; Toyoshima 2013, *furoku*, 2). In fact, long before the publication of *Sanctos*, Alessandro Valignano was already requesting the creation of a type for kana syllables to be used for printing in a letter dated 25 December 1584. Wicki (1975, 762) provides a transcript of the text in *Documenta Indica*, vol XIII.
9 This comparison clearly shows the stylistic similarities between those used in *Sanctos* (①75, ②148) and those used in Pinadellus (1589).
10 In *Sanctos* these marks were used to emulate the internal subdivision of the source text. An example is given in Table 2.4. A similar use of this section marker can be seen in the table of contents of later *kirishitanban* printed with Japanese scripts, in which the symbol § was used together with the character *dai* 第 to mark the beginning of subsections within a chapter (e.g. 第一§一, 第一§二, … = #1.1, #1.2, …).
11 See López-Gay (1959) for more information on the first Jesuit library in Japan.
12 López-Gay (1959, 374) further suggests that *Cathalagus Sanctorum* could have been *Flos Sanctorum*.
13 See the section 'Sanctos as an example of cultural translation' for a full translation of the note to the reader.
14 A detailed description of translation strategies adopted in *Sanctos* will be provided in the following section.
15 See Pereira (2008) for a study of book illustrations as (intersemiotic) translation.
16 The Latin passage may be a misquotation from James 4:6 or Peter 5:6 rather than Isaiah.
17 Pia Jolliffe thanks fray Julián de Cos and Orii Yoshimi for our exchanges on Luis de Granada. All translations from Spanish, Portuguese and Japanese in '*Sanctos* as an example of cultural translation' are produced by Pia Jolliffe.
18 In the early seventeenth century, the Jesuits also published Chinese translations of *Introduction del symbolo de la fe* in Macao. These were prepared by the Dominican Friar Thomas Mayor in Manila (Beckmann 1968, 202).
19 It was common to use 'm' and 'n' interchangeably (Ruiz-de-Medina 1995, 535).

Bibliography

Anonymous (1591) *Sanctos no gosagueo no uchi nuqigaqi*. Kazusa: Iesus no Companhia no Collegio.

Beckmann, J. (1968) Luis de Granada in chinesischer Übersetzung. *Zeitschrift für Missionswissenschaft und Religionswissenschaft* 52: 200–203.

Breen, J., and Williams, M. (1996) *Japan and Christianity: Impacts and responses*. Basingstoke: Macmillan.

Brower, R.A. (2014) *On translation*. Cambridge, MA: Harvard University Press.
Clements, R. (2015) *A cultural history of translation in early modern Japan*. Cambridge and New York: Cambridge University Press.
de Cos, J. (2020) Email to the author, 7 August.
de Granada, L. (1583) *Segunda Parte de la Introduction del symbolo de la fe*. Çaragoça: Domingo de Portonarijs Ursino.
de Sande, D. (1590) *De missione legatorum Iaponensium ad Romanam curiam*. (*Macaensi portu Sinici regni*) Macao: Jesuit Press (In domo Societatis Iesu).
Devonshire, J.T., Murray, L., and Murray, P. (eds.) (2013) *The Oxford dictionary of Christian art & architecture*. 2nd ed. Oxford: Oxford University Press.
Espinosa, A. (2013) Luis de Granada, 1504–88. In: Karla Pollman (ed.) *The Oxford guide to the historical reception of Augustine*. Oxford: Oxford University Press.
Emmerich, M. (2013) *The tale of Genji: Translation, canonization, and world literature*. New York: Columbia University Press.
Emmerich, M. (2014) Translating Japanese into Japanese: Bibliographic translation from woodblock to moveable type. In: Bermann, S. and Porter, C. (eds.) *A companion to translation studies*. Chichester: Wiley-Blackwell.
Farge, W.J. (2009) Translating religious experience across cultures. In: Üçerler, M.A.J. (ed.) *Christianity and cultures*. Roma: Institutum Historicum Societatis Iesu.
Fróis, L. (1942) La Première Ambassade du Japon en Europe, 1582–1592. In: J.A. Abranches Pinto, Yoshitomo Okamoto and S.J. Henri Bernard (eds.) *Première partie: le traité du Père Fróis. Ouvrage edité et annoté par J.A. Abranches Pinto, Yoshitomo Okamoto and Henri Bernard*. Tōkyō: Sophia University.
Fróis, L. (2002) *Historia de Japam*. CD-ROM. Lisbon: Comissão Nacional para as Comemorações dos Descobrimentos Portugueses (Ophir- Biblioteca Virtual dos Descobrimentos Portugueses; 10).
Fujikawa M. (2017) Studies on the Jesuit Japan Mission. *Jesuit Historiography Online*. Last accessed on 22 December 2020 http://ezproxy-prd.bodleian.ox.ac.uk:2197/10.1163/2468-7723_jho_COM_196472
Fukushima, K. (1979) *Santosu no gosagyō: honji-kenkyūhen*. Tōkyō: Benseisha.
Genette, G.R. (1997) *Palimpsests: Literature in the second degree*. Lincoln: University of Nebraska Press.
Higashibaba I. (2001) *Christianity in early-modern Japan: Kirishitan belief and practice*. Leiden: Brill.
Hisashi, K. (2009) From Dainichi to Deus. In: Üçerler, M.A.J. (ed.) *Christianity and cultures*. Roma: Institutum historicum Societatis Iesu.
Huerga Teruelo, Á. (2018) Fray Luis de Granada. *Real Académica de la Historia*. Last accessed 9 November 2020. http://dbe.rah.es/biografias/11233/fray-luis-de-granada.
Ignatius of Loyola (1996) *Personal writings*. London: Penguin.
Jakobson, R. (1959) On linguistic aspects of translation. In: Brower, R.A., and Fang, A. (eds.) *On translation*. Cambridge, MA: Harvard University Press.
Kaiser, S. (1996) Translations of Christian terminology into Japanese, 16–19th centuries: Problems and solutions. In: Breen J. and Williams M. (eds.) *Japan and Christianity*. Basingstoke: MacMillan Press, 8–29.

Kishino, H. (2009) From Dainichi to Deus: The Early Missionaries' Discovery and Understanding of Buddhism. In: Ucerler, M.A.J. (ed.) *Christianity and cultures: Japan & China in comparison, 1543–1644*. Roma: Institutum Historicum Societatis Iesu.

Kōso, T. (2006) *Sanctos no gosagveo no vchi nvqigaqi*. Tōkyō: Yūshōdō Shuppan.

Laures, J. (1957) The Jesuit Mission Press in Japan. *Monumenta Nipponica* 13(1/2): 163–165.

López-Gay, J. (1959) La Primera Biblioteca de los Jesuitas en el Japón (1556). Su Contenido y su Influencia. *Monumenta Nipponica* 15(3/4): 350–379.

Loureiro, R.M. (2006) Alessandro Valignano and the Christian Press in Japan. *Revista de Cultura* 19: 134–153.

Miyazaki, K. (2003) Roman Catholic mission in pre-modern Japan. In: Mullins, M. (ed.) *Handbook of Christianity in Japan*. Leiden: Brill, 1–18.

Moran, J.F. (1992) *The language barrier and the early Jesuits in Japan*. Stirling: The Scottish Centre for Japanese Studies.

Obara, S. (1996) *Santosu no gosagyō*. Tōkyō: Kyōbunkan.

Orii, Y. (2010) *Kirishitan bungaku ni okeru Nichi-Ō bunka hikaku: Ruisu de Guranada to Nihon*. Tōkyō: Kyōbunkan.

Orii, Y. (2011) *Hidesu no kyō*. Tōkyō: Kyōbunkan.

Orii, Y. (2015) The dispersion of Jesuit books printed in Japan: Trends in bibliographical research and in intellectual history. *The Journal of Jesuit Studies* 2(2): 189–207.

Orii, Y. (2021) Email to the author, 13 January.

Pacheco, D. (1971) Diogo de Mesquita, S. J. and the Jesuit Mission Press. *Monumenta Nipponica* 26(3/4): 431–443.

Pereira, N. (2008) Book illustration as (intersemiotic) translation: Pictures translating words. *Meta: Journal des Yraducteurs* 53: 104–119.

Pinadellus, J. (1589) *Inuicti Quinarij Numeri series*. Romæ: Apud Franciscum Zannettum. (Bodleian Library, Vet. F1 e.314).

Ruiz-de-Medina, J. ed. (1995) *Documentos del Japón 1558–1562*. Rome: Institutum Historicum S.I.

Ruiz-de-Medina, J. (2003) The role of the blind *Biwa Hōshi* troubadours in the history of the Christian mission in Japan. *Bulletin of Portuguese-Japanese Studies* 6: 107–145.

Rumiko, K. (2009) The adaptation of the sacraments to Japanese culture. In: Üçerler, M.A.J. (ed.) *Christianity and cultures*. Roma: Institutum Historicum Societatis Iesu.

Satow, E.M. (1888) *The Jesuit Mission Press in Japan, 1591–1610*. London: Priv. print.

Schurhammer, G. (1928) *Das kirchliche Sprachproblem in der japanischen Jesuitenmission des 16. und 17. Jahrhunderts*. Tōkyō: Deutsche Gesellschaft für Natur- und Völkerkunde Ostasiens.

Schütte, J.F. (1940) Christliche Japanische Literatur, Bilder und Druckblätter in einem unbekannten vatikanischen Codex aus dem Jahre 1591. *Archivum Historicum Societatis Iesu* IX(2): 226–280.

Schwemmer, P. (2014) My child Deus. Grammar versus theology in a Japanese Christian devotional of 1591. *Journal of Jesuit Studies* 1: 465–482.

Sobczyk, M. (2016) *Higashi Tōjirō kyūzōbon "Kirishitan shōmono" no kenkyū: Sekkyō to no kakawari o chūshin ni.* Torún: Wydawnictwo Naukowe Uniwersytetu Mikołaja Kopernika.

Sobczyk, M. (2020) Estrategias de domesticación y extranjerización en la traducción al Japonés de Tratado de la Oración y Meditación. In: Yoshimi, O. and Calvo, M.J.Z. eds. *Cruces y Áncoras. La Influencia de Japón y España en un Siglo de Oro Global.* Madrid: Abada Editores, 159–177.

Takao, M.H. (2019) 'In their own way': Contrafactal practices in Japanese Christian communities during the 16th century. *Early Music* 47(2): 183–198.

Teresa of Avila. (2002) *The complete works*, vol. 1. London and New York: Burns & Oates.

Triplett, K. (2018) The Japanese Contemptus Mundi (1596) of the Bibliotheca Augusta: A brief remark on a new discovery. *Journal of Jesuit Studies* 5: 123–127.

Tominaga, M., and Tenri Toshokan. (1973) *Kirishitanban no kenkyū.* Tenri: Tenri Daigaku Shuppanbu.

Tominaga, M. (1978) *Kirishitanban monjikō.* Tenri: Tominaga Makita Sensei Ronbunshū Kankōkai.

Toyoshima, M. (2013) *Kirishitan to shuppan.* Tōkyō: Yagi Shoten.

Ucerler, M.A.J. (2008) The Jesuit enterprise in sixteenth- and seventeenth-century Japan. In: Worcester T. ed. *The Cambridge companion to the Jesuits.* New York: Cambridge University Press, 153–168.

Üçerler, M.A.J. (2009) *Christianity and cultures: Japan & China in comparison, 1543–1644.* Roma: Institutum Historicum Societatis Iesu.

Ucerler, M.A.J. 2010) Missionary printing. In: Suarez, M.F and Woudhuysen, H.R. (eds.) *The Oxford companion to the book.* Oxford: Oxford University Press, 107–115.

Walsham, A. (2016) Luis De Granada's mission to protestant England: Translating the devotional literature of the Spanish counter-reformation. In: Bela T., Clarinda C., and Rzegocka J. (eds.) *Publishing subversive texts in Elizabethan England and the Polish-Lithuanian commonwealth.* Leiden: Brill, 129–154.

Ward, H.N. (2020) Women, households, and the transformation of Christianity into the Kirishitan religion. In: Nadine A. (ed.) *Catholic missionaries in early modern Asia.* Abingdon and New York: Routledge, 176–189.

Wicki, J. (1956) O "flos sanctorum" do P. H. Henriques, impresso na língua tamul em 1586. *Boletim do Instituto Vasco da Gama* 73: 42–49.

Wicki, J. (1975) *Documenta Indica 1583–1585*, vol. 13. Romae: Apud Institutum Historicum Societatis Iesu.

Yanaike, M. (2003) *Yokogaki tōjō: Nihongo hyōki no kindai.* Tōkyō: Iwanami Shoten.

3 The making of the Korean Bible

A case study of James S. Gale's New Testament and Genesis translations

Jieun Kiaer and Kyungmin Yu

Introduction

This chapter sketches a brief history of the Bible in Korean and the writers and translators involved in its creation. We show how early Protestant missionaries played an important role in establishing vernacular grammar and speech styles during a time of flux in the Korean language. At the time, from the late nineteenth to the early twentieth century, the Korean language was undergoing a variety of changes due to changes in the social structure, the popularisation of Korea's indigenous alphabet Hangeul and Western influences—particularly that of English.

We shall focus on the role James Scarth Gale (1863–1937) played in the making of the Korean Bible as well as the Korean language itself. As we will discuss in Section 3, Gale's achievements have not been widely recognised until recently.

We will explore these issues using a case study of Gale's Korean Bible (1925), focusing on how he used his creativity to adapt the text to resonate with Korean readers by considering the particularities of the Korean language and culture. For example, he incorporated Korean Neo-Confucian values such as filial piety into the text, as well as innovating a new Korean term for 'God,' *hana-nim* (Lit. 'one' + respect particle), taking advantage of the Korean honorific system in order to succinctly express the monotheistic nature of Christianity. We shall discuss three characteristics of Gale's translations and their impact on the making of the Korean Bible.

Bible translators and missionary grammarians

A fact that one cannot help but admire throughout the Far East, one which does not flatter our self-esteem, is the presence of books in even the poorest homes. Those who cannot read are very rare and incur the scorn of their fellow citizens. We would have a lot of people to despise in France if public opinion against the illiterate were as severe here.

(Henri Zuber, *An Expedition in Corea*, 1873)

Korea has long been a highly literate nation with a great enthusiasm for reading and studying, and the written word was hugely important in spreading Christianity throughout Korea. Until 1784, the few Christians that were in Korea had used Bibles imported from China, which were written in Classical Chinese, the common linguistic capital in pre-modern East Asia at the time. However, Koreans wanted their own Korean Bible. As such, producing an easy-to-read translation of the Bible in Hangeul became a priority for Western missionaries hoping to spread Christianity in Korea, and work on translating the Bible into Korean began even before missionaries entered the Korean peninsula. This was a highly unusual situation, as Reynolds writes:

> When the American missionaries, Revs. H. G. Underwood, H. G. Appenzeller and W. B. Scranton passed through Japan, they were given a few copies of St. Mark's Gospel in Korean, which they had in their hands when they landed at Chemulpo in 1885. This was one of the few cases in the history of Missions where the missionaries reached the country in which they were to labor, carrying with them God's Word in the language of the people.
>
> (Reynolds, 1910–1911, 296)

Indeed, when the first missionaries arrived in Korea in 1885, they arrived carrying Korean copies of Mark's Gospel, which had been translated into Korean by Yi Sujeong (1842–1886) published in Yokohama, Japan.

The first complete translation of the Bible into Korean, however, was translated by the Scottish Presbyterian missionary John Ross (1842–1915) and his team, who were stationed in Manchuria (present-day Northeast China). Ross' translation was completed in 1887 and imported into Korea. Ross worked with his brother-in-law John Macintyre (1837–1905) and four Korean men from Uiju, a county in North Pyongan Province in present-day North Korea: Yi Ungchan, Baek Hongjun, Kim Jinki and Yi Seongha. Later, Ross also met Seo Sang-ryun (1848–1926), who was born as a member of the *yangban* nobility but lost his parents at the age of thirteen and became a *ginseng* merchant. When he was in Manchuria at the age of thirty-one, he caught typhoid fever but survived thanks to Macintyre's help. From this point on, Seo became a committed Christian, joined Ross' translation team, and even went on to establish the first Korean church, *Sorae Kyohoe* ('Sorae Church').

Ross' translation was influenced by the regional and occupational backgrounds of his Korean assistants, and as a result the text uses North-western Korean dialect, which was an issue for future revisers of the Bible, who thought the dialect sounded unsophisticated, preferring a more 'neutral' form of language. This did not prevent Ross' translation from finding huge success, however. The translation sold out of its initial pressing, and between 1883 and 1886 'no less than 15,690 copies of [Ross' translation] were circulated in Korea through three colporteurs.' Indeed, it was such a success that Reynolds considers the Ross translation to have 'laid the foundation' of missionary work in Korea (Reynolds 1910–1911, 302–303). There was a huge demand for the Korean Bible, and this would only continue to grow: according to Hwang and Yi (2012, 8), over 16 million Bibles were published between 1895 and 1934. Seeing this demand, the mission board became very supportive of efforts to translate and publish Bibles in Korea.

The process of creating and distributing Korean Bibles was also expedited by a strategy that was hugely influential on missionaries from the late nineteenth to the early twentieth century: the Nevius Method, which was pioneered by the American Presbyterian missionary John Livingstone Nevius (1829–1893). One of the key principles of the Nevius Method was for missionaries to provide the locals with copies of the Bible in their own tongue. This also meant that the Bible should be written in a vernacular style that would be broadly accessible, and so in the case of Korea, the Nevius Method clearly specified that all religious texts should be written in *Joseon mal* Korean vernacular' alone (Clark 1930).

Individual translation (1887–1898): collaboration between western missionaries and Korean *josa*

Like many other early missionaries, Gale also worked closely with his Korean colleagues, or *josa* ('helpers') such as the Korean intellectual Yi Changjik (1866–1938), with whom he was close friends. Gale's friendship with Yi is clear from the passage below:

> For eight years I had in my employ a young man who had been born with some means, and so had not learned to work. He had spent his life at school in the study of Chinese. I first met him in a little hut on the seashore many miles from the capital. He had an attractive manner that took my fancy, and I asked him if he would come with me. He agreed, and we made our first visit to Fusan together. Other natives had warned me against him, as being easily led into bad company, which was true, in a way; but notwithstanding this defect, in all the eight years never once did he deceive or fail me. He was ever ready to sacrifice his own

comfort or convenience to mine; would give extras from his table in his desire that I should fare well; would lay his few treasures, whatever they might be, at my feet, if he thought they could be of use; was insulted and abused for standing for my honor - and yet, faithful in everything for eight long years, as far as his relationship to me and those around me was concerned, his was the most faultless life I have ever seen.

(Gale 1898, p. 241-242)

It was compulsory for missionaries at the time to take Korean language courses for three years, followed by an exam to check their progress. After passing the exam there was no need to continue studying Korean, but Gale had so many books he wanted to translate that he employed Yi for eight years until 1897. At first, Yi worked as Gale's assistant, but later he was listed as a co-translator in many of Gale's works (Yi 2000, 170).

Ross and his team

Initially, Bible translation was carried out by small teams formed of English-speaking Western missionaries and their Korean helpers, *josa*, who worked in close collaboration. The missionaries did not just rely on *josa*, however; the missionaries themselves also studied Korean fervently, as we shall return to in the section 'Case Study: James Gale's Bible.'

Ross' translation of Luke's Gospel was first published in Korean in 1882. This version was translated into North Western dialect, but in their subsequent translation of John's Gospel, they incorporated elements of both North Western dialect and Seoul dialect according to Macintyre. From Mark's Gospel onwards, Ross' team aimed to translate into Seoul dialect, yet despite this some dialect words remained, such as *abam* 'father' and *omam* 'mother.'

The translation process used by Ross' team is also worthy of note. Firstly, the *josa* on Ross' team would translate the Chinese Bible (1852) into Korean, which Ross and Macintyre would then compare with the Greek and English translations to check the meaning was preserved. Ross's translations aimed to be as literal as possible while still conveying the appropriate meaning in a colloquial style. It was in Ross' translation that the word *hanunim* or *hananim* was first used to translate 'God' into Korean. This was a new word formed by combining *hanul* 'heaven' and *-nim* 'lord, respect particle.' This was a departure from the word used in the Chinese Bible, s*angje* (上帝) or *sin* (神).

This word for 'God' is very similar to what Gale would later use; however Gale was more successful in justifying his use of the word to other missionaries, and it was Gale who popularised *hananim*. Gale's *hananim* was derived from the root 'one' rather than 'heaven,' emphasising the monotheistic nature of Christianity. We shall return to this in the section 'Missionary Literature in China, Greater China, and Taiwan.' Ross argued that he chose the word to help the Joseon people identify the Christian God with their existing beliefs of a deity reigning in Heaven—allowing them to reconcile Christianity with their pre-existing religious and spiritual beliefs. Although creating continuity with Koreans' existing beliefs was not a bad idea, his word *hanunim* or *hananim* (literally 'dear Heaven') sounded too superstitious and animistic to other missionaries at the time; in other words, there was perhaps too much continuity with native Korean religion for it to catch on. The first Scriptures in Korean, the Gospel of Luke and the Gospel of John, were published in Manchuria (present-day China) by Rev. Ross and his Korean colleagues with the support of the National Bible Society of Scotland (now the Scottish Bible Society), which was based in Korea from 1883–1887. It was Seo Sang-ryun who first brought these translations of the Gospels into Korea (Yi 2020).

Although Joseon Korea was within the 'Sinosphere' and had a tradition of using literary Chinese, Ross' team avoided using many of the Chinese words and terms used in the Chinese Bible, opting instead to adapt such terms to fit with the Korean language and culture. They understood that the Korean language has its own unique Sino-Korean words that do not exist in Chinese—equally, many Chinese words are not used in Korean. Translators made the necessary adjustments in order to produce a Bible that would appeal to Korean readers.

The board of revisers and official translation

Eventually, however, this era of individual translations gave way to a more organised system. The Korean branch of the Bible Society was founded in Korea in 1905 under the name the 'Korean Agency of the British and Foreign Bible Society' (BFBS). The same system of close collaboration between English-speaking missionaries and Korean *josa* was used even after translation became more organised, however.

Interestingly, despite many French Jesuit missionaries arriving in Korea from France beginning in the 1840s, French Jesuits did not participate in Bible translation in this period, despite publishing many influential books such as *Dictionnaire Coréen-Français* and *Grammaire Coreenne* (1881).

A timeline of Bible translations

In this section, we will provide a simple timeline of the different stages of Bible translation. Reynolds (1910–1911, 302–303) classifies these stages as follows:

62 *The making of the Korean Bible*

Figure 3.1 The Board of Translators of the New Testament (Pyongyang, 1904). (Back row) Kim Chung-sam, Kim Myong-jun, Yi Chang-jik (Front row) W.D. Reynolds, H.G Underwood, J.S Gale. (Source: Underwood 1918).

a) Efforts from without the Hermit Nation, 1865–1887.
b) Individual versions by various missionaries, 1887–1898.
c) Production of the Official Board's Version of the New Testament, 1897–1904.
d) Authorized Translation of the Old Testament, 1904–1910.

Individual translations

Table 3.1 presents a history of individual translations of the Bible predating the Board and official translations.

Board translations

> *Punyuk ta toyusso* was the message flashed over the wires from the Chunju section of the Board of Official Translators of the Scriptures Saturday evening, April 2nd, 1910, announcing to the Agent of the British and Foreign Bible Society at Seoul, Korea, the glad tidings that the task of translating the whole Bible into the Korean language had been completed.
>
> (Reynolds 1910–1911, 292–293)

Table 3.1 History of Bible translation (individual translations)

Year of publication	Translators	Publication(s)
1882	John Ross and his team	Luke's Gospel, John's Gospel
1883	John Ross and his team	Luke's Gospel, Acts
1884	John Ross and his team	Matthew's Gospel, Mark's Gospel
1884	Yi Su-jeong	Mark's Gospel
1887 (translation happened in Korean Peninsula)	H.G. Appenzeller, H.G. Underwood	Mark's Gospel
1891	Malcolm C. Fenwick	John's Gospel (Revised Ross and his team's version)
1892	H.G. Appenzeller	Matthew's Gospel
1892	J.S. Gale	Acts
1895	H.G. Underwood	Luke's Gospel
1895	J.S. Gale	John's Gospel, Acts
1897	W.B. Scranton	James
1898	W.D. Reynolds	Thessalonians
1898	W.B. Scranton	Romans
1898	W.B. Scranton	Hebrews

After the formation of the Board of Revisers, translations of the Bible became more regulated, and the process of translation also became more orderly. From this point, the Board began publishing official translations, beginning with the Old Official Translation, followed by the Revised Official Translation and then the Revised Re-Officialised Translation, which started to be widely used from 1961. Table 3.2 presents a timeline of the different editions published by the Board.

The problems of *Joseon Mal-ro* 'into the Korean vernacular'

Joseon mal and Hangeul

The Nevius Method proposed translating into the Korean vernacular, or *Joseon mal*. However, the precise meaning of what constitutes *Joseon mal* or the Korean vernacular is not so easy to define, as we will return to in the section 'Case Study: James Gale's Bible.' The Nevius Method focused on the 'unlettered'—non-aristocrats who lacked the privilege to study literary Chinese. However, a more informal or vernacular written style had not yet been established; although Hangeul existed it was not widely used, and ordinary people did not know how to use it effectively. Because of this,

Table 3.2 The making of the Korean Bible

Official translation	Revised official translation	Revised re-officialised translation
New Testaments (1906a)	Old Testament (1936)	1998—this is the version that is used in South Korea now
New Testaments Korean-Chinese hybrid version (1906b)	Old Testament Korean-Chinese hybrid version (*Seonhanmun*) (1937)	
Old Testament (1911)	New Testament (1938)	
Bible - including both Old and New Testaments (1911)	New Testament Korean-Chinese hybrid version (*Seonhanmun*) (1940)	
1912–1936 *Seonhanmun*	Bible—including both Old and New Testaments (1938)	
	Bible—including both Old and New Testaments easy Korean-Chinese hybrid version (1961)	

there was no existing framework of written 'Korean vernacular' to serve as a model for translating into *Joseon mal*. As such, translators had to experiment with different styles to find an effective way of expressing vernacular language in writing.

For more than 450 years since its initial conception in 1446, Korea's indigenous script was treated with little reverence, in contrast to Classical Chinese, which was the prestigious form of language for many centuries. It was only in 1894 that it received its status as the 'national' script, or *gukmun* (國文). This was enacted by King Kojong (1852–1919), who published a special order in 1894 decreeing that all laws and regulations should be published in the national script rather than Classical Chinese (*hanmun*, 漢文). This was one part of the Gabo reform (1894–1896) marking the transition from Joseon to the Korean Empire, which included striking changes such as the abolition of the class system and the adoption of Hangeul as the national script. Under this new decree, Classical Chinese would only accompany Hangeul when strictly necessary. This was revolutionary for the fate of Hangeul, which gained a newfound prestige as the national script. *Hanja*, or Chinese characters, were still very much in use. For this reason, it would still be some time before the use of pure Hangeul became commonplace.

It would also only be a few years before Hangeul once again lost its status as *gukmun* upon the Japanese annexation of Joseon in 1910. Japanese authorities established Japanese as Korea's new national language and script. In these unfortunate circumstances, a new term for Korea's indigenous writing system became necessary.

The making of the Korean Bible 65

The following is an account from *The Independence* endorsing the first Korean-English dictionary, written by Gale. In the article by Seo Jaepil (1864–1951), he refers to the Korean alphabet as both *Joseon mal* and *Joseon keulja*.

For Koreans who want to better learn *Joseon-mal* ... we hope you will buy this book and begin to study *Joseon-mal* first. The American teacher Gale took several years to create this dictionary of the Korean and English languages, and it was published just yesterday. It was sent from Japan to Seoul, and the final page count is around one thousand three hundred. Beneath the Korean, Chinese characters and English are provided, and at the end of the book important references are provided. This is the first time something this great has been made available in Joseon, and now that it has been created surely it will be met with words of praise and gratitude by not only the people of Joseon, but the people of the world. Because it was made in a truly academic way, it will certainly be useful to the people of Joseon and foreigners as well. It teaches both English and Korean, so that a Korean person can better learn the Korean language through it, and better learn to write in the *Joseon-geulja*. How could this not be a great event for our country? *The people of Joseon, even after living here for thousands of years, have not learned to a high degree their own language, and therefore must we not be grateful that the American teacher has made this book?* For Koreans who want to better learn *Joseon-mal,* as well as Chinese characters and English, we hope you will buy this book and begin to study *Joseon-mal* first.

(*The Independence*, 24 April 1897; my emphasis)

Missionary grammarians

Many Protestant missionaries, including Gale, also wrote Korean grammars alongside their Bible translations. As they translated, they often had to experiment with new styles and terms or reuse existing terms with new meanings; in this sense, we think it is more suitable to use the term *making* than *translating* to describe the process of creating Korean Bibles.

Some of the key works on the Korean language produced by missionaries in Korea are listed below:

1. Ridel 1880: Les Missionnaires de Coree, de la Société des Missions Étrangères de Paris, de Paris, (*Dictionnaire Coreen-Francais*), Yokohoma: C. Levy Imprimeur-Libraire, 1880.
2. Underwood 1890: Underwood, Horace Grant, (*A Concise Dictionary of the Korean Language*), Yokohama: Kelly & Walsh; London: Trubner & Co., 1890.

3. Scott 1891: Scott, James, *English-Corean dictionary: being a vocabulary of Corean colloquial words in common use*, Corea: Church of England Mission Press, 1891.
4. Gale 1897: Gale, James Scarth, (*A Korean-English Dictionary*), Yokohama: Kelly & Walsh, 1897.
5. Gale 1911: Gale, James Scarth, (*A Korean-English Dictionary*), Yokohama: The Fukuin Printing CO., L'T., 1911.
6. Jones 1914: Jones, George Heber, (*An English-Korean dictionary*), Tokyo, Japan: Kyo Bun Kwan, 1914.
7. Gale 1914: Gale, James Scarth, *(A Korean-English dictionary (The Chinese Character)*), Yokohama: The Fukuin Printing CO., L'T., 1914.
8. Gale 1924: Gale, James Scarth, (*Present day English-Korean: three thousand words*), Seoul, 挑戦耶蘇教書會 ('Korean Christian Reading Group', my translation), 1924
9. Underwood 1925: Underwood, Horace Grant & Underwood, Horace Horton, (*An English-Korean Dictionary*), Seoul, 挑戦耶蘇教書會 ('Korean Christian Reading Group', my translation), 1925.
10. Gale 1931: Gale, James Scarth, (*The Unabridged Korean-English Dictionary*) Seoul, 挑戦耶蘇教書會 ('Korean Christian Reading Group', my translation); 1931

As we can see, Ross, Underwood (1859–1916), and Gale are among those Bible translators who also published Korean grammars or dictionaries. Under the Nevius plan, all missionaries had to spend time mastering *Joseon mal* and *Joseon keulja/munja*: spoken and written Korean. However, as previously mentioned, a vernacular writing style had still not been established at this point, and these missionaries were therefore not only learning the Korean alphabet but also helping to shape it as they experimented with vernacular writing styles in their Bible translations.

From the late nineteenth to early twentieth century, Korea was a linguistic melting pot, in which new linguistic capital such as English entered the peninsula and large numbers of new words made from Chinese characters resulted in an influx of Sino-Korean words. Meanwhile, the indigenous Korean script took on a new status as the 'national' script. Concepts relating to Korea's 'modernisation' required new words, many of which were translations of English words.

The terms used to refer to Korea's indigenous alphabet were similarly chaotic during this period, and many terms for the alphabet co-existed from the late nineteenth to mid-twentieth century. This was also the case for many new conceptual terms used during this period—it was a time of great linguistic innovation, and not all of the new terms would stick. New words did not simply replace synonymous older terms, but rather both remained in use until usage settled, often in favour of one term or the other. Note that even standard orthographic conventions were not established until 1933.

In the Joseon dynasty, only yangban aristocrats were able to learn and use literary Chinese. It is said that it took the average yangban around twenty years to master literary Chinese to a satisfactory level, an amount of disposable time unthinkable for commoners. The less privileged classes of society needed a practical, pragmatic writing system that was easy to both learn and use. Hangeul was invented as a way to solve these twin problems of social injustice and linguistic inefficiency. Yet even after its invention in 1443 and promulgation in 1446 CE, Hangeul did not receive proper recognition in pre-modern Korea. Despite its functionality and convenience for encoding spoken Korean, Hangeul was denigrated by yangban literati, who advocated for literary Chinese as the only true script (眞書), arguing that its use was necessary in order to maintain Korea's self-defined national identity as 'little China' (小中華); by moving away from the Chinese notion of civilisation they risked being labelled as 'barbarians.'

Case study: James Gale's Bible

James Scarth Gale

James Scarth Gale was a prominent missionary in Korea. He was born in Ontario, Canada, in 1863 and studied Modern Languages at the University of Toronto before moving to Korea as a missionary with the YMCA in the same year of his graduation in 1888. Gale was a gifted linguist and quickly acquired an understanding of the Korean language far more sophisticated than his peers. He used his knowledge of Korean to publish numerous dictionaries and grammars for the language, such as *Sakwajinam* ('Korean Grammatical Forms') (1894) and *A Korean-English Dictionary* (1897). His interests were not limited to hard linguistics, however; Gale also had a keen artistic sensibility and an appreciation for Korean literature. As well as translating the Bible and works of English literature into Korean, he also translated Korean works into English, such as *The Cloud Dream of the Nine* by Kim Manjung (1637–1692), making him a bidirectional translator—somewhat of a rarity.

After marrying Harriet E. Gibson in 1892, he went on to collaborate with her and his Korean colleagues on an illustrated Korean edition of John Bunyan's *The Pilgrim's Progress* (Seoul: Trilingual Press), which was published under the title *Tiyeonroyeokjeong* (天路歷程) in 1895. The edition featured illustrations by the artist Kim Junggeun that adapted the original illustrations into a Korean style, making the text more approachable for Korean audiences—something that would foreshadow Gale's naturalising approach in his future translations. Gale was a key figure in translating the Bible into Korean, and he left behind a great impact and legacy.

Pragmatic translation

Hangeul was crucial for missionaries as it enabled them to actively engage with the Korean locals, translating to and from Korean with ease. Furthermore, in the early twentieth century, the Bible's translation into Hangeul played a crucial role in promoting and popularising Hangeul. Hangeul also conveyed ideas of modernism, allowing people of all linguistic backgrounds to access and communicate via the Korean language with relatively little training. This chapter gives an overview of the use of Hangeul in modern education methods in the Korean peninsula.

Despite the convenience of Hangeul, however, there were some advantages to Hanja, and some translators, including Gale, experimented with a hybrid style that maintained the use of Hanja for some words. Although Gale recognised the advantages of Hangeul, he was pragmatic enough to recognise the expressive potential of using Hangeul and Hanja together.

From the late nineteenth to early twentieth century, writing styles were in flux in Korea. Before the Gabo Reform at the very end of the nineteenth century, the official writing system was Hanmun or Kukhanmun. Hangeul was still used, but never in an official capacity, and it went underappreciated. In this linguistic environment, then, missionary translators had some freedom regarding what style to choose for their translations. They believed that the Bible should be written in accessible language, so they often favoured using Hangeul.

Gale was not only skilled in the Korean language, but also Chinese. He published a highly sophisticated reader of Chinese characters, *Yumongcheonja* (牖蒙千字, *The Thousand Character Series. Korean Reader*), which was so ahead of its time in recognising which Chinese characters were the most essential that its content overlapped 93% with the list of 1,800 characters set to be taught in schools by the Korean Ministry of Education in 1972 (Lee et al. 2017).

In contrast to most other missionary translators, who wrote in pure Hangeul, Gale utilised his knowledge of Chinese, writing using a mixed script that incorporated both Hangeul and Hanja. Gale realised that foreign Biblical concepts carried little resonance with Korean readers when simply transliterated from English using Hangeul and recognised that by using Hanja he could tie otherwise foreign concepts into Korean readers' existing framework of knowledge, which was greatly influenced by Chinese concepts.

Writing Korean using a hybrid script has a long history. When Hangeul was first promulgated, one of its primary purposes was to facilitate the understanding of hanmun, serving as a gloss. Hanmun was the sole literary script for the yangban nobility, most of whom were desperate to maintain their monopoly over erudition; they had no incentive to abandon this prestigious script in favour of purely using Hangeul. Hangeul was added to publications of key Neo-Confucian works during the Joseon period, and it was also used to raise awareness of diverse areas of knowledge, such as Buddhism, medicine, and science. However, King Sejong never intended Hangeul to replace hanmun and become the sole script. He simply intended to create a writing system accessible to people from all classes and backgrounds. He wanted to convince his scholars of the efficacy of a hybrid style where Hangeul could be used as a useful medium in understanding Classical Chinese texts.

Korean native scholars had also experimented with hybrid writing styles but these were difficult to use and understand for the general public. For example, Yu Seongjun (1860–1934) and Yu Kiljun (1856–1914)—the latter of whom wrote the famous Seiyukyeonmun (西遊見聞, 'Observations on Travels in the West')—played important roles in exploring hybrid styles using a combination of Hangeul and Hanja, influencing later hybrid Bibles. However, the Yu brothers were members of the nobility and wrote in an erudite style that was inaccessible to the general public. This kind of mixed script, featuring both Hangeul and literary Chinese, was called *Kukhan-mun* (國漢-文) or *Seonhan-mun* (鮮漢-文). The latter term was often used after the Japanese annexation of Korea, as during Japanese occupation the term *kuk* ('country') came to refer to Japan. As such, this part of the word was replaced with *seon* (鮮), a character often used to refer to Joseon Korea.

In comparison to the hybrid styles adopted by Korean elites, Gale aimed to use a more vernacular hybrid style that could be read by a far broader audience. In pioneering this style for his new Bible translation, he believed that it was essential to find a good balance between Hangeul and Hanja.

One might question why Gale did not decide to write exclusively in Hangeul if he was aiming for accessibility, given that modern Korean is written almost entirely in Hangeul, with Hanja being used only rarely. However, in Gale's time a Hangeul-only policy was not ideal for several reasons. Firstly, Hangeul writing was still not well-established; many religious and philosophical texts were still written and read in Classical Chinese. Furthermore, the logographic nature of the Chinese script helped aid understanding of new or unfamiliar concepts, as one can often infer the meanings of a Hanja compound from the meaning of the constituent characters; in contrast, an unfamiliar word written in Hangeul often provides no hint to its meaning. Gale's hybrid style followed clear rules: pure Korean words would be written in Hangeul, while Sino-Korean words would be written in Classical Chinese. This served to maximise the accessibility and comprehensibility of the text, as there was nothing to impede understanding of familiar Korean words, while Hanja provided hints to the meaning of more complex or unfamiliar Sino-Korean words. This approach of maximising comprehensibility and accessibility by using a mixed script is perhaps reminiscent of Hangeul's earlier role as a gloss for Hanja.

The pragmatic use of Hanja has a long history in Korea. From the seventh century, scribes used Hanja to write pre-modern Korean by alternately using characters for their semantic or phonetic content. For example, a Hanja with a particular meaning in Chinese might be read out loud as the Korean word with the same meaning, or in other cases, a Hanja with a particular sound in Chinese might be used to represent part of a Korean word that features that same sound. Representing Korean sounds using the rough Korean pronunciations of Chinese characters was a rather clunky system, however, and so it made perfect sense to use Hangeul for this purpose instead due to its excellent phonetic expressive power, while still maintaining the use of Hanja for their semantic content.

Gale recognised that Korea at the time was highly influenced by Chinese thought and language. In the following passage, he makes clear the degree to which he believed Korean language and culture were intertwined with that of China, justifying his decision to use a mixed script that maintained continuity with Chinese ideas:

> Such being the nature of these centuries of Chinese influence Korea has to-day no life, literature or thought that is not of Chinese origin. She has not even had a permanent Manchu occupation to break the hypnotic spell of Confucianism. Even her language, while possessing a basis of form entirely different from that of China, has had the latter language so grafted into it, and the thought of the same so fully made a part of its very essence, that we need the Chinese character to convey it. This will account for the native contempt of the native script. *En-mun (諺文) has become the slave of Han-mun (漢文)*, and does all the coolie work of the sentence, namely, the ending, connecting and inflecting parts, while the Han-mun, in its lordly way, provides the nouns and verbs. Out of a list of 32,789 words, there proved to be 21,417 Chinese and 11,372 Korean, that is twice as many Chinese as native words. At the present time, too, the language is being flooded by many new terms to represent incoming Western thought, and these are all Chinese.
>
> (Gale 1900. My emphasis.)

Essentially, Gale was attempting to improve on existing modes of expression while still maintaining continuity with Chinese ideas which he felt were central to Korean ways of thinking. Although modern Korean is written almost entirely in Hangeul, in Gale's time, people had still not learned to use Hangeul properly on its own; after all, it took 450 years after the

The making of the Korean Bible 71

invention of the Korean script for it to become official and be promulgated. By mixing elements of the familiar and the unfamiliar, Gale was able to innovate while still expressing ideas in a natural and comprehensible way.

Translating key terms

When they began the work of translating the Bible into Korean, missionary translators were faced with a huge number of new concepts, terms, and names that lacked any direct Korean equivalent. Due to the huge phonetic expressive potential of Hangeul, it was of course possible to directly transliterate religious terms into Korean unchanged. This was useful for names and place names, but when terms and concepts were transliterated in this way, the end result became confusing and difficult to read. Some translators, however, were far more aware of the importance of considering the reader when translating. These translators took a naturalising approach, using more creative, indirect translations to produce a text that read almost as if it had originally been written in Korean.

When Gale was working on his Korean translation of the Bible, the issue of how to translate the word 'God' was a difficult one. Rather than transliterating the word from English or using words associated with Korean religion, which may have resulted in confusion, Gale decided on the word *hananim*, which roughly means 'the one Great One.' This word is etymologically related to 'heaven,' but Gale has adopted this word to mean 'one' with the same form. The word consists of the word 'one' followed by a respect particle, expressing the fact that there is only one God in Christianity. As mentioned before, this was similar to the word Ross used, *hanunim*; however Gale's word was related to the other meaning: 'one' rather than 'heaven'—this set it apart from native Korean religions while also communicating the monotheism of Christianity.

This more circuitous approach, taking advantage of Korean's nuanced honorific system, illustrates the kind of creative approach that is often necessary for the most natural translations. Below is a quotation from a conversation between Gale and Ju which shows how Gale's decision to translate 'God' as *hananim* in Korean was influenced by Ju Si-gyeong (1876–1914), who is often called the grandfather of Korean linguistics:

> 'Our God,' said Chu, 'is the great One, and is called by us *Hananim*, from the word *Hana*, meaning one, and *nim*, meaning lord, master, king. The one great Lord of Creation is *Hananim*. We associate him with the building of the universe (*Chun-ji*), and also call Him *Cho-wha-ong*, the ancient Creator.'
>
> (Gale 1900)

72 *The making of the Korean Bible*

See Oak (2013) for a more detailed discussion on Gale's adoption of the term *hananim*.

Order and hierarchy are very important in Korea due to the influence of Neo-Confucian ideology. In Ross' translation, however, honorifics and linguistic markers of interpersonal relations are omitted, as in English. Many conversations between Jesus and his disciples are translated without the use of any honorific expressions, for instance. This absence of honorifics and markers of respect sounds very unnatural in Korean.

For example, in John 2:4, Jesus calls his mother Mary 'woman'[1] in the English translation. Ross (1883) translates this term into Korean using the Korean word for 'woman,' as in English, which ends up sounding distant and unnatural. In contrast, Gale (1925) translated the term here as *emoni* 'mother:' a far more natural term to use here. This illustrates Gale's understanding of the nuances of the Korean language and his talent for naturalising translations.

Gale was a nuanced and creative translator—he did not simply find equivalent terms in Korean for English words but paid close attention to the nature of the Korean language, making use of honorifics and address terms to express a nuanced meaning that sounds natural in Korean. The speech styles used in Gale's 1925 Bible were highly influential, and their impact is still felt in the style of the contemporary Korean Bible (1998).

Many of the religious terms used in the Bible could be translated using existing Korean religious terms. For instance, theological roots such as *seong* (聖), *sin* (神), and gyeongbae(敬拜) existed before Christianity in shamanistic or Buddhist contexts. Words like *jabi* (慈悲) were solely used in Buddhist texts but are now also used in Christian contexts too. As the Bible became more and more influential in Korea, these roots are now often more closely associated with their Christian contexts. One

---

요한 02:04

예수 갈오디 부인은 나과 무삼 샹관이요 니 찌가 닐으지 못ᄒ엿나이다 ᄒ니 <1883년>
예수 갈오샤디 부인은 나과 무삼 샹관이요 니 찌가 닐으니 못ᄒ엿나이다 ᄒ니 <1885년>
예수 써 곧아샤디 여인과 나와 무슨 샹관 잇ᄂ뇨 니 찌가 이르지 아니ᄒ야짜 ᄒ시니 <1893년>
예수 써씌셔 곧ᄋ샤디 내가 녀인과 무슨 샹관 잇ᄂ뇨 내 째가 니르지 못ᄒ엿노이다 ᄒ시니 <1919년>
예수—곧ᄋ샤디 녀인이여 나와 무슨 샹관이 잇나잇가 내 째 아직 니르지 못하엿노이다 <1906년>
예수씌셔 갈아샤대 녀자여 나와 무삼 샹관이 잇나잇가 내 째가 아직 니르지 못하엿나이다 <1939년>
예수—곧ᄋ샤디 어머니여 나와 무슨 相關이 잇노잇가 내 째가 아즉 니르지 못ᄒ엿ᄂ이다<1925년>
耶穌曰,母我與爾何干,我時尚未至. <1889년>

Figure 3.2 A comparison of Korean translations of John 2:4.

additional advantage of maintaining linguistic continuity with native shamanistic and Buddhist terms is that it helps to familiarise what could otherwise be a foreign, confusing text. Gale presented many of the terms used in his Bible in Hanja. For example, the Korean word *buhwal* 'resurrection' first appeared in Mark 12:18 (1906a) written in pure Hangeul. However, in the Korean-Chinese hybrid version (1906b) and Gale's version (1925) the word is presented in Hanja as 復活. It is rather difficult to guess what *buhwal* means if one is not already familiar with the word, yet writing the word in Hanja makes the meaning much clearer. Gale's talent as a translator was evident in how he excelled not only at the technical work of translating but also in considering the best orthography with which to convey the translation. For example, by using *hananim*, the meaning 'one' could be introduced to the term *hananim*, adding a new nuance to the word.

Controversial translation: translating the Bible

> And if any man shall take away from the words of the book of this prophecy, God shall take away his part out of the book of life, and out of the holy city, and from the things which are written in this book.
> (King James Bible, Revelation 22:19)

Translation can often be controversial even for the most seemingly innocuous of texts, yet nowhere is this more true than when translating religious texts such as the Bible. As demonstrated by the above quotation from the Book of Revelation, the stakes are far higher: any alteration to the text will apparently be met with divine punishment, denying one access to Heaven. Many have interpreted this and other similar passages as an in-text demand for a faithful approach to the Bible's translation. The translator's own soul is not the only one that hangs in the balance, either: the missionaries believed that by converting Koreans to Christianity they were saving their souls from purgatory or hell, and an inaccurate translation of the Bible that failed to communicate the correct teachings would fail in this task. One prominent member of the Board, Horace Underwood, put it explicitly as follows:

> for with a book like the Bible where the turn of a single phrase, nay the definition of a single word – may affect the eternal destiny of thousands of souls ... the original shall be [as] perfectly conveyed as it possibly can be in the medium used.

In light of this, it is easy to see why Gale's translation of Genesis inspired such heated arguments.

This has significant implications for Bible translations: anything deviating from the most literal approach can easily be criticized as a betrayal of the text or even of God, even when such changes would result in a smoother or more natural target text. Gale was often criticized in these terms, being treated almost as if he were trying to sabotage the text. In a letter to Miller discussing Gale's text, Adams wrote that 'One would almost think that the translators, whoever they were, thought that they were able to express the Lord's thoughts better than He, himself' (277). In another letter, Erdman criticizes Gale's decision to omit one mention of God when he translated the passage 'He called the name of the place where God spoke to him, Bethel' as 'He called the name of the place Bethel' in Korean (249). Gale justified the decision citing his Korean assistant who told him that the mention of God 'adds nothing' to the thought. Erdman sarcastically comments that 'it seems to me that it merely adds GOD to the thought, which is of considerable value to the theologian though it may not be to the literati!' (249) In this way, Gale is treated by many of the other missionaries as if he is intentionally attempting to make the text less holy or remove God from the text.

Erdman's slightly derogatory characterization of Gale as a member of the 'literati' rather than a theologian brings us to another theme of the heated debate between Gale and Miller—the question of who is qualified to assess the quality of a translation of the Bible. To Miller and his supporters, who tend to value traditional church institutions and qualifications, Gale's lack of formal theological training (he studied the arts, rather than theology, at university) serves as further evidence that he lacks the knowledge or respect for the text necessary to properly translate it. Yet Gale, with his artistic sensibilities and deep understanding of Korean, found his approach criticized by missionaries with far less fluent Korean and little appreciation for the nuances of translation. Gale harshly describes Miller as having 'no knowledge of practical translation work' and living 'purely in the world of theory and yet without sufficient experience to have even that right' (237). In other words, both parties believed that their own area of expertise alone made them best suited to assess the translation.

Translations of the Bible have been treated with trepidation and suspicion for a long time. In 1408, the Archbishop of Canterbury, Thomas Arundell, made clear his concerns about the consequences of liberal or unauthorized translations of the text in his *Constitutions of Oxford*, stating:

> It is a dangerous thing, as witnesseth blessed St. Jerome to translate the text of the Holy Scripture out of one tongue into another, for *in the translation the same sense is not always easily kept* ... We therefore decree and ordain, that no man, hereafter, by his own authority translate

any text of the Scripture into English or any other tongue … and that no man can read any such book … in part or in whole
(Moynahan, *God's Bestseller*, xxii; my emphasis)

From the above, it is clear that Arundell feared that vernacular translations of the Bible risked distorting the holy messages of the text. Yet he also acknowledges that translation is an imperfect process where 'the same sense is not always easily kept;' equivalence in translation, where both form and meaning are perfectly preserved between languages, is an impossibility. Arundell's solution to this dilemma was to demand strict oversight over future translations, prohibiting anybody to translate the text 'by his own authority,' and banning the reading of any such unauthorized translations.

The Official Board of Translators seems to have been based on a similar philosophy. The final translation was to be arrived at democratically, preventing any one person from altering the text too much 'by his own authority'—at least in theory. Missionary translators held regular meetings at which they went through their work verse by verse, considering the suggestions and criticisms of the other translators. Finally, the best translation was to be decided upon by majority vote (Kim 2016, 67). Whether or not this process was effective, however, was another matter. Gale was accused of attempting to force through his translation regardless of the opinions of the other Board members—he was accused of 'railroading' by Dr. Reynolds and of having an 'unwillingness to listen' (258).

Gale's translation was eventually blocked by the Board, however. Even after resigning from the Board of Official Translators in 1923 and privately publishing his translation in 1925, church officials managed to effectively block its distribution. It garnered almost no readership, Gale having essentially been silenced by the missionary community (Kim 2016, 74).

Faithfulness vs. naturalisation

At the core of Gale and Miller's dispute over Gale's translation is a conflict between faithfulness and naturalisation in translation. Miller's priority was of course to preserve the integrity of the source text as much as possible. To him this meant replicating every last detail from the English in the Korean text, even down to the word. On the other hand, Gale's approach was to naturalise the text to accommodate the needs of the register: he worked closely with his Korean colleagues, listening to their criticisms and suggestions to ensure that the text would read almost as if it were originally written in Korean. To Gale, a smooth style and an accurate translation were not mutually exclusive: he felt that the changes necessary to adapt the text into smooth Korean did not detract from the 'whole meaning' of the text but rather brought the text closer to this goal. Gale made his approach clear as follows: 'My greatest ambition is to have the Book speak the thought, no more and no less, but to speak it in sweet easy-flowing Korean' (Rutt, 1972, 72).

Looking at the arguments Gale makes defending his translation in his letter to Dr. Kilgour, his naturalising approach is very clear. He points out Miller's lack of interest in the feedback of native Koreans in favour of that of missionaries:

> Mr. Miller treats very lightly the Korean side of the Board. We have three men, experienced translators, two have served over twenty years and one over ten. They know their language and can handle it with consummate skill. Mr. Miller could by no means claim such a mastery of English.
>
> (Oak 2013, 238–239)

He goes on to argue against the rigidly faithful approach favoured by Miller, stating that 'In days gone by the Korean let all sorts of expressions pass into the text on the understanding that they belonged to the original and could not be changed' (239). This inflexible approach is what Miller is essentially arguing for, yet Gale points out that a previous translation that took this approach resulted in 'Yi Wun-mo, our most skillful linguist, saying to himself in a distressed way as he read a paragraph preparatory to revision, "Dear me, like the ravings of a drunken man!"' In a letter to Koons, Coen also mentions that some previous Bible translations had prioritised faithfulness so much that they rendered words that lacked straightforward Korean translations into 'an anglicized hybrid tongue,' 'slavishly follow[ing]' the English text rather than attempting to find more natural Korean analogues (234). Clearly, previous translations that attempted to maximise faithfulness failed to find a balance between faithfulness and the style and aesthetic value of the target text.

Here, the benefits of Gale's naturalising approach are clear: surely a highly literal, faithful translation that sounds like 'the ravings of a drunken man' or relies on confusing English loanwords risks destroying the reader's connection with the text, something that is essential for a text like the Bible—especially when the goal is to convert readers to Christianity. Miller and Gale's other critics felt that something of the Bible would be lost if omissions or small alterations were made. Yet Gale recognised that it was more important that readers were moved by the text, rather than being reminded of 'the ravings of a drunken man.' In other words, to Gale, the style and aesthetic qualities of the text were as much a part of the Bible as its semantic content, and both aspects of the text needed careful attention to ensure a good experience for readers.

Linguistic differences

Although issues of faithfulness and naturalisation were at the heart of the controversy over Gale's translation, these terms are not so easy to define when two languages differ as much as English and Korean. In a long letter to Dr. Kilgour defending his translation, Gale points out that many of the changes criticised by Miller can be explained by the fundamental differences between the English and Korean languages. He argues that these omissions are not mistakes, oversights or intentional attempts to cut from the text but are rather simply the most natural way of expressing the source meaning in natural, grammatical Korean. Indeed, Korean and English have vast differences in terms of linguistic features, or 'feature inventories.' As Gale explains, '[I would] render every sentence, every phrase, every word just as they appear in the original if the Korean language would in any way permit it. But orderly grammatical Korean we must have ...' (Oak 2013, 239). In other words, the linguistic differences between Korean and English call into question the notion of a 'faithful' translation, as attempts to literally translate a Korean work into English will result in ungrammatical or awkward language, necessitating a more creative, but less straightforwardly 'faithful' approach.

One of the criticisms made of Gale's translation along these lines was his supposed omission of the word 'God:' Gale recounts Erdman's proposition that 'as the name of God appears twenty-eight times in the Hebrew of the first chapter of Genesis it ought so to appear in the Korean' (238). Gale recounts that upon hearing this, Dr Reynolds 'simply smiled at the suggestion.' This is because Korean is a highly context-dependent language; information that is clear from context need not be directly specified. Because of this, it can often appear as if words present in the English source text disappear in the transition to Korean. The crucial point, however, is that this does not necessarily result in the loss of any information. This may seem counterintuitive, but it makes sense when we consider that the English language often requires us to specify redundant information—the Korean language simply allows us to avoid needlessly repeating this redundant information, leaving it implicit instead. In Gale's words,

> [Erdman] did not realize that in Korean, under certain circumstances, a repetition suggests not the same but another subject of the same name. So the Korean asks, as I have on more than one occasion heard, 'Is it another God you are speaking of?' 'Why, no!' 'Then don't repeat the subject here.' Mr Engel also pointed out to the Bible Committee very

> correctly that while the name for God appears only ten times in the Korean there are fifty-two honorific forms that run through the chapter making the subject perfectly clear to the reader.
>
> (238)

As Gale illustrates, the omissions of the name of God are not truly omissions, in that the numerous honorific forms running through the text make the meaning just as clear to the reader as if the word God had indeed been repeated in every instance.

Even if the meaning is preserved, however, there are still some valid criticisms that could be made about Gale's approach here. For instance, if one feels that the repetition of the word 'God' serves a poetic function, the text would of course lose that meaning if 'God' were rendered indirectly using honorifics. In a letter to Miller, Allen Clark raises this issue, saying that 'I've always felt that the continual repetition of the name of God there was intentional, to drive home the fact of his immediate agency' (266). Stanley Soltau expressed a similar sentiment to Miller, saying that using honorifics rather than directly repeating the word 'God' 'weakens the force and the authority of the text,' and that his Korean secretary

> says that while there is no question as to who is referred to by the constant use of the honorific form of the verb, it nevertheless is not so strong as the old version where the word for God is repeated no less than 30 times.
>
> (262)

While these are valid criticisms, they do not show that Gale was mistaken in his approach. In any translation, there are hundreds of decisions to be made about which meanings to prioritise carrying over from the source text, and the question of whether to express God as the subject of verbs through honorifics or the word 'God' comes down to personal preference in the end; some translators may feel the poetics of the repetition is more important, while Gale evidently thought the smoothness of the honorific approach added more to the text. In other words, though valid, it seems short-sighted for Miller to use these criticisms, which boil down to stylistic preference, as evidence of the unfaithfulness of Gale's translation.

Despite their heated arguments, however, Gale seemed to believe his friendship with Miller would survive despite their strongly divided opinions, writing:

> Now that I am very keen to trouble you with such a long letter as this. If it does not appeal to you just drop it into the waste-paper basket and say no more about it. Mr. Miller and I shall be just as good friends as

ever, both priding ourselves on the fact that we have Scotch in us, and so have a right to differ in opinion at times.

(Oak 2011, 245)

If we are to believe Gale's words here, perhaps he also had a more good-natured side, in addition to the fiery temper often described in accounts of his behaviour.

Conclusion

In summary, Korea has a long history as a highly literate nation, and missionaries were quick to capitalise on this with a string of Bible translations beginning even before missionaries set foot in the country. However, entrenched aristocratic preference for Classical Chinese, as well as a general state of linguistic flux in Korea at the time, meant that there was no good pre-existing template for writing the Korean language in a style accessible to a broader audience beyond the aristocracy. The Nevius mission strove to translate the Bible into the Korean vernacular, or *Joseon mal*, yet as there was still little tradition among Koreans of writing down Korean as it was spoken; even this vernacular style had to be pioneered by missionaries experimenting with various styles. Translators such as Gale attempted to keep continuity with existing writing traditions by taking a pragmatic approach, using a mixed script which played to the advantages of both Hanja and Hangeul. By keeping continuity with Chinese ways of thinking through the use of Hanja, it was also possible to translate foreign Christian ideas and terms within the framework of existing religious ideas, calling back to Korean readers' existing knowledge of shamanistic and Buddhist traditions in order to easily communicate the otherwise unfamiliar concepts of Christianity. Despite the calls of the Nevius mission for missionaries to translate into vernacular Korean, however, Gale faced intense criticism when he attempted to translate the Book of Genesis using a naturalising approach, resulting in his eventual resignation from the Board of Revisers and the denial of an audience for his privately published translation in 1925.

Note

1 'Woman, why do you involve me?' Jesus replied. 'My hour has not yet come.'

Bibliography

Cawley, K. (2017) *Religious and philosophical traditions of Korea* (1st ed.). London: Routledge.

Clark, A.C. (1930) *The Korean Church and the Nevius methods.* New York: F. H. Revell.
Gale, J. (1894) *Sakwajinam.* Seoul: Trilingual Press.
Gale, J. (1897) *A Korean-English dictionary (한영자뎐).* Yokohama: Kelly & Walsh.
Gale, J. (1898) *Korean sketches* (1st ed.). New York, Chicago, and Toronto: F. H. Revell Co.
Gale, J. (1900) Korean ideas of god. *The Missionary Review of the World*, September.
Heo, J. (2012) Hangugeo gyoyuksaui gwanjeomeseo bon gyorinsujiwa sagwajinam bigyo yeongu (A comparative study of KYORINSUJI and SAGWAJINAM from the viewpoint of Korean education). *Hanmaryeongu* 31: 361–384.
Hong, S. (2008) *Naming God in Korea: The case of protestant christianity.* Oxford: Regnum Books, 99.
Hwang, H., and Yi, S. (2012) Gaenyeomgwa yeoksa, geundae hangugui ijungeosajeon. In *Concepts and history, Modern Korea's bilingual dictionary: The modernity of Korean language with respect to the foreign missionaries' dictionary making.* Seoul: Bangmunsa.
Kiaer, J. (2020) *Pragmatic particles.* London: Bloomsbury.
Kim, W. (2016) James Scarth Gale as a translator. *Korea Journal*, 56: 32–60. 10.25024/kj.2016.56.2.32.
Lee, S. (2017) Tracing the origins of Hangul and of Hunminjeongeum (『訓民正音』) – Westerners' theories about the origin of Hunminjeongeum as recorded in "The Korean Alphabet" (1912) by James Scarth Gale. *Korean Language and Literature in International Context, Gukjeeomun (International Language Study)* 72: 7–48.
Moynahan, B. (2003) *God's bestseller: William Tyndale, Thomas more, and the writing of the English Bible---A story of martyrdom and betrayal.* London: Little, Brown.
Noss, P. (2007) *A history of Bible translation.* Rome: Edizioni de storia e letteratura.
Oak, S. (2011) Historical documents of the Korean Bible society, vol. III. *Correspondence of Hugh Miller* (1st ed.). Seoul: Korean Bible Society.
Oak, S. (2013) *The making of Korean Christianity: Protestant encounters with Korean religions.* Waco: Baylor University Press, 1876–1915. Available from: ProQuest Ebook Central. [14 November 2020].
Rutt, R. (1972) A biography of James Scarth Gale. In R. Rutt (ed.) *James Scarth Gale and his history of the Korean people.* Seoul: Royal Asiatic Society Korean Branch, 1–88.
Underwood, L.H. (1918) *Underwood of Korea: Being an intimate record of the life and word of the Rev. H. G. Underwood, D.D., L.L.F., for thirty-one years a missionary of the Presbyterian Board in Korea.* New York: Fleming H. Revell Co.
Yu, K. (2019) *Seonggyeonggwa hangugeo* (Bible and Korean). Jeonju: Jeonju University Press.
Yu, K. (2020). *Gidokgyo yongeoui beonyeokgwa sasangui tochakwa yeongu (A study on the naturalisation of translation and thought in Christian terms: Focused on the Korean translation of the Jesus and the God) Urimal Yeongu.* Seoul: Korean Linguistic Society, vol. 60, 115–139.
Zuber, H. (1873). *Une expédition en Corée, 1866. Le Tour du monde: Nouveau journal des voyages.* Paris and London: Hachette, 25: 401–416.

4 A translation designed to guide

Campbell N. Moody's *Pėh-ōe-jī* or Romanised Minnan Taiwanese *New Vernacular Translation of and Commentary on Romans I-VIII* (1908)

Kazue Mino

Introduction

In modern Protestant foreign mission endeavours, literature constituted its integral part. Based upon the belief that the word of god is the foundation of the Christian faith, various mission societies placed great emphasis on the distribution of literary works. In the case of early missionaries in China and Greater China, a focus on the production of Christian literature in native languages was made, urged on not only by this agenda of their own but also by the Qing dynasty's prohibition on open evangelism before the mid-19th century (Zhang 2005, 75; Bays 2012, 43). Interdenominational cooperation was actively made in the process, and the well-known debates over the choice of translation of certain key words such as 'God,' and the different translations of the bible, such as the Delegates' Version (1855) in *Wen-li* or classical Chinese and the Union Version (1919) in Mandarin vernacular, were created through the collaboration of missionaries across different affiliations (*Records of the General Conference* 1878, 207, 210; Bays 2012, 49).

Accordingly, in 1865, when the Presbyterian Church of England (PCE) had commenced its work in Taiwan, which was then situated in the periphery of the Qing Empire, they soon began to prepare for the construction of a printing facility. The Book Room, equipped with a printing press, was opened in 1884 at their headquarters in Taiwanfu (present-day Tainan), and the next year saw the inauguration of *Tâi-oân-Hú-siâⁿ Kàu-hōe-pò* (*Taiwan Capital Church News*, hereafter, *the Church News*), a monthly periodical written in the missionary-devised Romanised Amoy Vernacular, or Minnan Taiwanese, called *Pėh-ōe-jī* (POJ). Their notable literary contributions

DOI: 10.4324/9781003032342-4

include *A Dictionary of the Amoy Vernacular Spoken Throughout the Prefectures of Chin-chiu, Chiang-chiu, and Formosa* (1913) by William Campbell (1841–1921) and the revised translation of the POJ *New Testament* (1916) and *Old Testament* (1933) by Thomas Barclay (1849–1935) (Lai 1988c).

However, the multi-linguality of those lands demanded that missionaries deliberate over which style, language and written form should be employed to make those publications as clear, simple and effective as possible. As most of the population of the Empire, except for the ruling elite, had no command of classical language in Han characters, it was also a question about their target readers: whom the missionaries were attempting to address, or rather, for whom these Protestant missionaries were being sent in the first place. In other words, it was a missiological question closely pertaining to their perception of themselves, the potential and actual converts and the dynamics between them. Accounts of interdenominational debates indicate that full agreement upon such a problem was not easily achieved. Divergence was also witnessed within each mission society, and PCE missionaries in Taiwan, while agreed in their aim to evangelise the masses through POJ, still made varied stylistic choices when producing their literature. Moreover, in the case of biblical translation, it is of particular importance to note that missionary translators' choices of written style were firmly linked to their own expectations about not only the target readers' ability to understand the words of god but also to the universality and/or limitation of the biblical message itself.

In this context, Campbell N. Moody's (1865–1940) *Lô-má-phoe*, or formally, *Lô-má-phoe I kàu VIII chiu^n Sin Hoan-èk ê Pèk-bûn í-kìp Tsù-kái, Kóe-seh, Káng* (*New Vernacular Translation of and Commentary on Romans I-VIII*, Tainan 1908), is a noteworthy subject by which to examine the case of a missionary translator in Taiwan. The relatively unknown yet unique partial translation of the epistle is significant for its clear intention to guide Taiwanese readers to what Moody himself, another PCE missionary, considered to be a sound and proper theological understanding of the Christian faith. In this light, *Lô-má-phoe* is also notable for its sharp contrast to the renowned Barclay Version bible, the aforementioned revised POJ scripture, which expressly aimed to provide an accurate translation of the biblical text for Minnan speakers. Thus, in order to understand the historical context of biblical translation in Taiwan and the significance of Moody's *Lô-má-phoe* within it, a two-tiered analysis will be carried out in this chapter. First, a broader framework of the questions faced by missionary writers and translators in the realm of the former Qing Empire, or China and Greater China, will be outlined, and the history of POJ literature in Minnan-speaking regions will be summarised. This chapter will

A translation designed to guide   83

then examine how Moody's attitude towards Taiwanese converts, his missiological standpoint, his approach to biblical texts and the interrelationship among these are reflected in *Lô-má-phoe*, with particular reference to their contrast with those of the Barclay Version.

Missionary literature in China, Greater China, and Taiwan

Questions regarding the range of the target readership and the method of producing effective literature for such readers had been debated among the missionaries in the Qing Empire from a fairly early stage. In 1877, the first General Conference of Protestant missionaries in China was held in Shanghai (Tiedemann 2010, 52), during which a heated discussion regarding the following problems was had: who should be the target readers, the masses or the literati, what style should be taken, classical or colloquial, what language should be the standard, Mandarin or another vernacular and what script should be employed, Chinese or Roman characters?

In many cases, divergence among the participating missionaries was due to the regional variation of their mission fields, including the extent of influence of the literati in each locality. Thus, the same attempt to make their literary works effective had led some to emphasise that it is essential to prepare *Wen-li* literature in Han characters for the literati, while prompting others to maintain a concentration on the works for the commoners through literature in their spoken languages. For the former, *Wen-li* literature had the potential not only to enable a dialogue with the educated and influential class but also to reach out to the literate population across the vast domain of Greater China and the Sinosphere including Korea, Manchuria and Japan. For the latter, communication with the masses counted not only in terms of numbers but also because of their somewhat romantic Protestant self-recognition that the gospel was for '[t]he unlearned and the poor,' the people they were specifically called to champion. Others, especially those who worked in Mandarin-speaking regions, argued that the production of literature in Mandarin in Han characters should be prioritised, for they believed that the already widely used vernacular would be the main language of the Empire in the future. On the other hand, for the missionaries who worked in Minnan-speaking regions, due to the fact that some sounds in the language cannot be notated with Han characters, the development of an alternative writing system that was easy to learn and that could be utilised by both missionaries and native Minnan speakers had been their main objective. As a result, the Romanised spelling was largely adopted, and thus at the

84 *A translation designed to Guide*

Conference a characteristically non-interventional and regionalist attitude was embodied in PCE missionary Carstairs Douglas's (1839–1877) straight denial of the utility of Mandarin literature in his mission field Amoy and the frank acknowledgement of its effectiveness elsewhere in the Empire (*Records of the General Conference* 1878, 220).

In the formation of a POJ writing system, a critical role was played by the missionaries of the London Missionary Society (LMS), who, before the opening of the Qing Empire, chose to work among the ethnic Minnan Chinese in Southeast Asia. For instance, Walter H. Medhurst (1796–1857) had compiled a Minnan vocabulary in 1820 with the hope of contributing to the evangelising works among the Minnan-speaking population in Malaya. After several additions and revisions, it was published in Macao in 1837 as *A Dictionary of the Hok-këèn Dialect of the Chinese Language*, of which the spelling system has been considered the prototype of POJ notation (Murakami 1968, 98). The later part of the nineteenth century saw a further systematisation of the spelling through several biblical translations and vocabulary compilations by the workers of LMS, which, after the First Opium War and the resulting treaties in the early 1840s, relocated their stronghold from Malacca to Hong Kong and treaty ports such as Shanghai and Amoy. Missionaries of the Dutch Reformed Church in America (DRCA) and PCE, which made their way into Southern China respectively in 1842 and 1847, also played a major part.

Early versions of Romanised Minnan bible renditions published around this time include *Iok Han Thoan Hok Im Su* (*Gospel According to John*, Canton 1852) by Elihu Doty (1809–64), *Lō-tek ê Chheh* (*Book of Ruth*, Amoy 1853) by John V.N. Talmage (1819–92), *Má-kó Hok-im Toān* (*Gospel According to Mark*, Amoy 1858) by Alvin Ostrom of DRCA, *Sú-tô Hêng-toān* (*Acts of the Apostles*, Amoy 1867) by John Stronach (1810–88) of LMS and *Lō-ka Hok-im Toān* (*Gospel According to Luke*, Amoy 1868) also by Talmage of DRCA (Lai 1988a; Tân 2015, 53). As for the lexicographical works during this period, *Chinese-English Dictionary of the Vernacular or Spoken Language of Amoy* (London 1873) by Carstairs Douglas, the aforementioned PCE missionary of Amoy, came to be known as one of the most authoritative repositories of POJ concordance.

Against this background, James L. Maxwell (1836–1921), the first PCE missionary to Taiwan, also started a translation of the bible within a few years of the initiation of his medical work on the island in 1865 (Maxwell 1871, 276). In cooperation with the PCE, DRCA and LMS missionaries in Amoy, Maxwell published *Lán ê Kiù-chú Iâ-so˙ Ki-tok ê Sin-iok* (*Our Lord Jesus Christ's New Testament*, Glasgow) in 1873. Under his supervision, the three missions then commenced a retranslation of the *Wen-li* Old Testament texts of the Delegates' Version into POJ, which resulted in the

1884 publication of *Kū-iok ê Sin-keng* (*The Old Testament*, London) (Lai 1988b). Thus, the translation of all of the POJ biblical texts was completed, yet immediately thereafter the need to improve the quality was strongly felt among those involved. Thus, another inter-society scheme to revise the POJ New Testament texts was launched in the same year, allotting different books in the bible to missionaries across Amoy and Taiwan for reworking. However, due to the difficulty in coordinating this undertaking, the plan did not succeed and was abandoned. Nearly thirty years passed before the next attempt at a revisional work on the POJ New Testament books was made in 1913 (Band 1936, 139; The Bible Society in Taiwan 2006).

Commissioned to this task was Thomas Barclay, a senior PCE missionary in Taiwan who was well known for his contributions to the aforementioned development in literary works, including the establishment of the Book Room. The revisional work was launched in Amoy in 1913 by Barclay and a team of three native translators, Lim Un-jin, Ng Ma-hui and Lu Lok-tia. Multiple versions of biblical texts were consulted, including 'the revised Greek Text,' 'various English translations' and Mandarin and *Wen-li* renditions in Han characters such as the revised Union Version, those of Griffith John and S.I.J. Schereschewsky and the Bridgman and Culbertson Version (Band 1936, 144). The first copies of their revised POJ New Testament were issued in May 1916 as *Sin-iok* (*The New Testament*, Yokohama), and about 60,000 copies were sold across Taiwan, Hokkien and Malaya during the next fifteen years (Band 1948, 158). In 1925, Barclay was then called by the British and Foreign Bible Society to retranslate the POJ texts of Old Testament books ('Missionary Paragraphs' 1925, 95), which was again taken up by the team in Amoy in 1927. Despite the serious impact of the Shanghai incident in 1932, during which their manuscript, which happened to be in the city awaiting printing, was destroyed amid the conflict between the Japanese and Chinese armies, Barclay managed to recreate the final manuscript through the use of the original manuscript and the semifinal proofs, and *Kū-iok ê Sèng-keng* (*The Old Testament*, Shanghai) was published in 1933. Thus, the revisional work on the entire POJ scripture was completed, and what came to be known as the Barclay Version bible made its way out into the world (Band 1936, 172). While criticisms have been made of its rigid style based on a literal translation of the original text into the type of Minnan that is more Amoy than Taiwanese (Lîm 2013), the Barclay Version has been widely used among the Presbyterian community in Taiwan and is still remembered as one of the best-known POJ bible renditions.

Moody's *Lô-má-phoe* (1908): its educational intention and bibliological view

In 1908, an attempt to produce a new Minnan Taiwanese bible translation of a noticeably different sort had been made in the form of *Lô-má-phoe* by Campbell N. Moody. Joining PCE's Taiwan mission at the dawn of the Japanese colonial era in 1895, Moody came to be known for his intensive direct evangelism, which included street preaching and outstation visitations in Mid-Taiwan. Being as much a prolific writer as an industrious preacher, Moody had multiple publications in English and POJ during and after his years as a missionary. Among those, *Lô-má-phoe* is the only extant POJ bible commentary produced by him. To clarify the aspects of this uncommon piece of biblical translation in the context of PCE's Taiwan mission, a threefold study of *Lô-má-phoe* will be carried out: (1) an examination of its bibliographic features and format, (2) an analysis of Moody's style of translation with particular reference to and comparison with that of the Barclay Version, and (3) a further comparative study on Moody's and Barclay's views on the nature of biblical text.

Designed for clarity and approachability: bibliographic features and format

In December 1908, a short article on the *Church News* announced the publication of *Lô-má-phoe*, stating that the book would provide 'a great help' for its readers in understanding the 'profoundly deep truth' addressed by *Romans* ('Cha̍p-sū' 1908, 111). The 120-page volume is composed of an acknowledgement, a preface and the main text with a notably unique format, to which Moody prompts the readers' attentions as follows: 'The method and order of this book need to be taken a little bit of notice. It should not be simply read through; if you do so, it won't make any sense.' The main text of the book has four separate yet mutually corresponding sections, all basically appearing on every double-page spread, which are as follows: (1) 'vernacular translation at the upper-left,' (2) 'commentary below it,' or at the lower-left, (3) 'explanation at the upper-right [which is] an interpretation of the vernacular translation,' and (4) 'discussions below explanation' at the lower-right (Mûi 1908, 'Acknowledgement'). Therefore, if one opens the first page of *Lô-má-phoe*'s main text, one would see the POJ translation of the first four verses of *Romans* chapter one in the upper half of that page and, at its bottom, a line separating the upper section from the lower half of the page, where a list of several keywords in bold typeface and short commentaries on each would be found.

For instance, in the upper section, one can read the first verse of *Romans* written as follows (Mûi 1908, 4):

A translation designed to guide 87

1. Iâ-so. Ki-tok ê lô-tsâi, siū-tiàu ê sù-tô Pó-lô, siū hun-phài khì thoân Siōng-tè ê hok-im (1. The servant of Jesus Christ and the called apostle Paul was separated and sent forth to propagate the gospel of God).'

Corresponding to this, four keywords, '*Iâ-so. ê lô-tsâi* (servant of Jesus), '*siū-tiàu ê sù-tô* (the called apostle),' '*siū hun-phài* (was separated and sent forth)' and '*Siōng-tè ê hok-im* (the gospel of God),' are listed in the lower section, along with explanations of the historical background and connotations of each. Thus, for the phrase '*Iâ-so. ê lô-tsâi*,' Moody provides commentary (Mûi 1908, 4):

> In the Old Testament, prophets are often called 'servant or server of Yahweh.' Paul followed suit with that expression, and replaced it with 'servant of Jesus.' By this, we can see that Paul looked upon Jesus as almost the same entity as God.

On the other hand, in the upper section of the next page on the right-hand side, one can find the corresponding 'interpretation' of the first four verses, among which, the very first reads as follows (Mûi 1908, 5):

> (1) Iâ-so Ki-tok ê lô-tsâi, hō I bóe, hō I siók, tåk-hāng hoa^n-hí hâng-hók tī I só-ài; iū-koh tsoè I ê chhe-eng, kap Pí-tek Iok-hān pî^n-pî^n chhit-iū^n siū-tiàu, chiū-sī Pó-lô, hō Siōng-tè lēng-gōa siat thang pò-iông I ê hó siau-sit [(1) Servant of Jesus Christ, the one who was redeemed by Him, the one who belongs to Him, and the one who happily surrenders to whatever that pleases Him; And the one who becomes His server, called just like Peter and John, that is, Paul, was separately set by God to propagate His good news].

Below a line at the bottom of this 'explanation' section, which separates the page into upper and lower parts in the same manner as the first page on the left-hand side, one would see the 'discussions' section, which provides some reasoning corresponding to the verses interpreted above, in a comparatively simple tone with numerous illustrations. Thus, in this page's case, a three-paragraph argument under the bolded title '*Iâ-so Ki-tok ê lô-tsâi* (servant of Jesus Christ)' is given, in which Moody points out that in the context of ancient Roman society, the word 'servant' actually indicated a slave, 'who was regarded as a property, not as a person' and whose life-and-death were all in their master's hands. He then continues that it should be noted that Paul, who must have been fully aware of this undertone as a

88   *A translation designed to Guide*

contemporary, consciously chose this expression and described himself as a 'servant' of Jesus, which points to the following implication (Mûi 1908, 5):

> (1) *We are purchased by Jesus* ... ; yet it is not by silver, but by His blood. (2) *Jesus purchased us, not to oppress us, but to set us free,* (from Hell, from the Devil, from sin, and from ourselves). (3) *Therefore, we willingly offer ourselves to become his servitors and servitresses.*

A no less detailed explanation of the background of the text of *Romans* is given in the preface, which reveals Moody's historical approach to the material. This can be also seen from the structure of the preface, which is developed through a series of bibliological themes as follows: (1) the City of Rome, (2) the Church in Rome, (3) When and to Whom *Romans* was Written, (4) the Cause for and the Purpose of this Epistle; and (5) Whether this Epistle was Truly Written by Paul and Truly Meant for Romans. Through this five-stage discussion, Moody sketches out some basic information on the epistle, such as the fact that ancient Rome was a city that thrived on the invasion of and colonial domination over the surrounding regions, that about 8,000 Jewish people were in the city at the time that Paul wrote the epistle and that it is written in Greek script. By referring to several studies in modern Western Europe (though without providing their bibliographic details), Moody also points out that it is believed that many of the members of the Church in Rome were 'gentiles' rather than Jews. He then introduces various theories regarding the time and place the epistle was written and Paul's purpose of writing it, as well as the question as to which part of it was genuinely written by Paul himself (Mûi 1908 'Thâu-sū [Preface]'). As seen, both the discussion and its historical and philological framework in the preface specify the character of Moody's attitude towards biblical text, which visibly reflects the method of modern bibliology.

While a detailed analysis of the style of the translated text will be carried out in the following sections, a quick glance at the characteristics of the commentary, interpretation and discussion parts should be mentioned here. First, Moody's writing is well organised and easy to follow owing to his method of developing discussion through various perspectives. This can be readily seen from some of the examples already quoted above, including the syllogism Moody adopts to explain the significance of the term '*Iâ-so͘ Ki-tok ê lô͘-tsâi*' in the discussion, as well as the preface, which is composed of five sections dealing with different historical aspects of the text of *Romans*. Three types of numbering are used throughout the commentary and discussion sections, with bolded Arabic numerals (**1.**, **2.**, **3.**, ...) as the first-tier separator, italicised bracketed Arabic numerals (*(1)*, *(2)*, *(3)*, ...) as

A translation designed to guide   89

the second, and italicised bracketed POJ syllables (*(b)*, *(ch)*, *(chh)*, ...) as the third-tier separator.

Second, with its frequent usage of exclamations and certain conjunctions, the text as a whole is written in fairly simple and approachable colloquial Minnan Taiwanese. For instance, exclamatory expressions such as 'Hó--lah! (Alright then!)' (Mûi 1908, 81) are used time and again in the commentary and discussion, and words such as 'O--ah (Wow)' (Mûi 1908, 61) are at times inserted into the passages in the explanation. Similarly, some conjunctions, such as 'Ta^n (Now then)' (Mûi 1908, 51, 63) and 'Sit-tsāi (Indeed)' (Mûi 1908, 33, 109), are added to the sentences in the interpretations, even though their corresponding passages in the translated texts do not contain those words. At the same time, Moody's constant use of questions and answers form in discussions also contribute to its readability. For instance, to clarify his point, Moody frequently deploys monologues such as 'What does the gospel speak about? It is about His Son' (Mûi 1908, 5); and 'Why am I [Paul] wishing gentiles to receive [surrender and have faith]? It is because I wish glory be to the name of Jesus' (Mûi 1908, 7). On one occasion, Moody takes it a step further and explains the passages he considers to be particularly difficult to tackle (1:1–8) through a fictitious debate between Paul and Jewish people critical of him, in which an ever so colloquial exclamation 'He! (Oi!)' is uttered by Paul (Mûi 1908, 31).

Third, the rich use of examples and anecdotes in the discussion section is another characteristic of Moody's writings. Such illustrations include stories that were considered to be familiar to the contemporary Taiwanese readers, such as a remark on the experience of going away to work in Singapore, Batavia and the gold mine of Gunung Ledang (Mûi 1908, 27), all of which were popular destinations for Minnan migrant workers at the time. Similarly, the name of Gô Béng 吳猛, one of the exemplars of *The Twenty-Four Paragons of Filial Piety*, a collection of stories depicting the Confucian values, well known across the Greater China regions, is mentioned in the discussion (Mûi 1908, 105). On the other hand, Moody also tells anecdotes that would have been considered rather new and exotic for most of the Taiwanese readers. These include a mention of the American Civil War (Mûi 1908, 63), as well as a story of how 'one girl in America, who fell ill and became blind, deaf, and mute at the age of 19 months old,' had always felt and sensed the presence of god (Mûi 1908, 19). While Moody never mentions this girl's name, the descriptions, including the girl's encounter with 'a very intellectual female instructor' at the age of eight, indicate that this is a story of the well-known American educator and activist Hellen Keller (1880–1968).

Thus, the bibliographic features and format of *Lô-má-phoe*, from its clear structuring to its usage of common colloquial expressions and anecdotes

90 *A translation designed to Guide*

both familiar and new to Taiwanese peoples, distinctly reveal Moody's aim to make it clear and approachable for his target readers.

A translation designed to guide: the style of body text

The newly translated Minnan Taiwanese vernacular text of *Lô-má-phoe* was by no means Moody's achievement alone. For '[t]o translate the text of *Romans* is truly a difficult challenge,' he needed the help of several native speakers, who were, 'the minister, Lîm Ha̍k-kiong [林學恭 (1857–1943)], evangelists Tiuⁿ Tō-sam [張道三 (1874–1933)], Tân Iú-sêng [陳有成 (1867–1934)], Ng Hiàn-chiong [黃憲章 (1878–1964)], Ng Tsok-pang [黃作邦 (1869–1907)], Ong Pôe-eng [汪培英 (1878-1949)] and Gô͘ Bí-kiàn [吳美見 (1882–1922)],' all to whom he expresses his gratitude (Mûi 1908, 'Acknowledgement'). They were fairly experienced evangelists well versed in biblical knowledge and POJ and Han character literacies, as well as having more than five years' practice in the field at the time of the publication of *Lô-má-phoe* ('Xili 1876 nian' 1957). Some of them, such as Lîm Ha̍k-kiong, were Moody's close colleagues, and their lives and personalities are vividly depicted in his English-based literature (Moody 1907, 1912, 1932). Contrary to this particular citation of his Taiwanese contributors, however, Moody does not mention which version of the bible the team had consulted. A comprehensive research of resources, covering an examination of POJ and Han character biblical translations, Greek text and English renditions published before 1908, is needed to address this question, which is well beyond the scope of the current chapter. Therefore, in what follows, an analysis specifically focusing on the different writing styles of Moody's vernacular translation in *Lô-má-phoe* and Barclay's *Sin-iok*[1], will be carried out. Concretely, three particular passages, namely, 2:7, 2:26 and 8:24, will be examined here. Table 4.1 shows Moody's and Barclay's POJ translations of the three verses, with the author's literal English translation of each added below them as references.

The first example, *Romans* 2:7 ('[T]o those who by patiently doing good seek glory and honour and immortality, he will give eternal life') shown in row (1), reveals that one of the most notable differences between Moody's and Barclay's renditions is the length of their sentences. This is due to the fact that whereas Barclay adopts much condensed phrases, Moody frequently employs explanatory and modifying expressions. For instance, to render the expression 'by patiently,' Moody chose to express 'bô siuⁿ-lán ti̍t-ti̍t kiâⁿ-hó ê hoat-tō͘ teh (by the method of tireless and continuous benefaction),' while Barclay simply expressed 'mî-nōa (patiently).' Similarly, the expression 'those who' is 'hiah-ê lâng (that person)' in Moody's rendering, while in Barclay's version, it is the third-person singular epicene pronoun 'i (them).' Another notable difference

Table 4.1 A comparison of the translated texts of *Romans* 2:7, 2:26 and 8:24 in Moody's *Lô-má-phoe* (1908) (Mûi 1908) and Barclay's *Sin-iok* (1916) (*New Testament Taiwanese Romanised Han Character Edition* 2004)

	Moody's *Lô-má-phoe* (1908)	Barclay's *Sin-iok* (1916)
(1) 2:7	[Ē]ng bô siūⁿ-lán tit-tit kiâⁿ-hó [ê hoat-tō˙] teh chhē êng-kng kap tsun-kùi kap bōe pāi-hoāi--ê, chiū hō˙hiah-ê lâng tit-tióh éng-oán--oáh. The person who seeks glory and honour and incorruptibility by [the method of] tireless and continuous benefaction, then that person will be made to acquire the everlasting life.	[K]ìⁿ-nā mî-nōa kiâⁿ hó, kiû êng-kng, chun-kùi kap bōe pāi-hoāi ê, chiong éng-oáh pò i. Every person who patiently does good, seeks glory and honour and incorruptibility, eternal life will be rewarded to them.
(2) 2:26	Án-ni bô siū kat-lé, nā siú lùt-hoat só˙-tēng ê gī, i-ê bô siū kat-lé kám bô thang sǹg sī kat-lé? Like that if [one] does not receive circumcision [but] keeps the righteousness that is set by the law, will not their uncircumcision be able to be counted as circumcision? [Yes they will be].	Só˙-í bô siū kat-lē ê nā siú lùt-hoat ê kui-lē, I ê bô kat-lé kiám bô beh sǹg-chòe kat-lé mah? So if those who are not circumcised keep the law's statutes, will not their uncircumcision be regarded as circumcision? [Yes they will be].
(3) 8:24	Taⁿ só˙ǹg-bāng--ê nā hō˙lâng khòaⁿ-kì chiū m̄-sī ǹg-bāng; in-ūi lâng nā teh khòaⁿ sím-mih, I siáⁿ-sū iáu teh ǹg-bāng [hit-ê mih]? Now if let [a] person see what they'd hoped for [,] then [it is] not hope; for if one saw something, how would they still hope for [that thing]? [No, they wouldn't].	Nā-sī í-keng khòaⁿ-kì ê ǹg-bāng, m̄-sī ǹg-bāng; in-ūi só˙khòaⁿ-kì ê, sím-mih lâng teh ǹg-bāng i? But hope that has been already seen, is not hope; for what has been seen, who would hope for it? [No one would].

between the two is the way they expressed the word 'give.' Moody chose to phrase 'chiū hō˙hiah-ê lâng tit-tióh éng-oán--oáh (then that person will be made to acquire the everlasting life)' by adopting the causative construction widely used in Minnan Taiwanese:

hō˙ + *object* + *verb* (*object* is made to *verb*)

On the other hand, without employing this syntax, Barclay phrased the same passage much simpler as 'chiong éng-oáh pò i (the eternal life will be rewarded to them).' In regard to the translation of this particular passage,

Lin Hsiang-Wei (2017) points out a resemblance between the usage of the word *bao* 報 in the preceding Han character bible renditions, which is in fact an equivalent to the term *pò* in Minnan Taiwanese, and the structure Barclay employed:

object₁ + pò + *object₂* (reward *object₂* with *object₁*)

For instance, in the first edition of the *New Testament* in Mandarin by Medhurst and John Stronach in 1857, the same passage reads '*jiu ba yong-sheng bao ta* 就把永生報他 (then rewards him with the eternal life),' using the exact same structure as the Barclay Version:

object₁ + 報/pò + *object₂* (reward *object₂* with *object₁*)

Similarly, in *The Holy Scriptures of the Old and New Testament in the Chinese Literary Language, Plain Style* by Schereschewsky (1902), it is rendered as '*ze bao yi yong-sheng* 則報以永生 (then rewards [him] with eternal life),' omitting one of the objects but still using a fairly similar structure:

報 [+ *object₂*] + 以 + *object₁* (reward [*object₂*] with *object₁*)

Based upon this observation, Lin (2017, 9) infers that it is possible that those Han character renditions had a certain influence on the Barclay Version.

Secondly, the passage in *Romans* 2:26 ('So, if those who are uncircumcised keep the requirements of the law, will not their uncircumcision be regarded as circumcision?') listed in row (2) also indicates notable differences between their phraseologies. For instance, in *Lô-má-phoe*, Moody rendered what is translated as 'the requirements of the law' in English as 'lu̍t-hoat só·-tēng ê gī (the righteousness that is set by the law),' by adopting the passive construction:

subject + só· + verb + ê + object (*object* that is *[passive verb]-ed* by *subject*)

On the other hand, Barclay chose to simply use a genitive case 'ê' and translated the passage as 'lu̍t-hoat ê kui-lē (the law's statutes).' Another noticeable difference between Moody's and Barclay's renditions of this passage is the latter's usage of the interrogative 'mah' at the end of the sentence. Since this is not entirely like Minnan Taiwanese phrasing, it

A translation designed to guide

is, according to Lin (2017, 14), another example of the influence of Han character bible renditions incorporated by Barclay, which can be compared to the translations of the same part in the Delegates' Version (1855) in classical Chinese (*qi bu-wei zhi yi ge hu* 豈不謂之已割乎 [why not call this already circumcised *hu*]) as well as in the aforementioned *New Testament* by Medhurst and Stronach (1857) in Mandarin (*qi bu-ke jiang ta dang-zuo yi ge de kan-dai ma* 豈不可將他當做已割的看待嗎 [why cannot give him the treatment for the already circumcised *ma*]).

Finally, the third example, *Romans* 8:24 ('Now hope that is seen is not hope. For who hopes for what is seen?') listed in row (3), also shows contrasts between Moody's and Barclay's styles of translation. For instance, to render the expression corresponding to 'hope that is seen,' Moody chose to compose the phrase 'só·ng-bāng--ê nā hō·lâng khòaⁿ-kì (let [a] person see what they'd hoped for)' that adopted the two aforementioned constructions: Namely, the passive {*subject* + só·+ *verb* + ê + *object* (*object* that is *[passive verb]-ed* by *subject*)} and the causative {hō·+ *object* + *verb* (*object* is made to *verb*)}. While the passive syntax here omits both the subject and the object, the subsequent context indicates that the sentence 'só·ng-bāng--ê' can be complemented as '[lâng] só·ng-bāng--ê [mih]' by adding the dropped subject 'lâng (person)' and object 'mih (thing).' Thus, in this sentence, Moody introduces a person who has a certain hope for something. Also, by using the causative syntax 'hō·lâng khòaⁿ-kì,' Moody depicts a scene in which this person is allowed to see what they had hoped for. In contrast, Barclay translates the same passage as 'í-keng khòaⁿ-kì ê ng-bāng (hope that has been already seen),' in which he simply explains the subject 'ng-bāng (hope)' as 'í-keng khòaⁿ-kì ê (that has been already seen).'

As seen from the three specific examples above, Moody's translation of *Romans* is characterised by his intention to guide the target readers to interpret the text in a certain way, or more precisely, to have an understanding of the scripture that is sound and correct in his eyes. The expositive style, aimed at providing every possible explanation to the words, and the adoption of constructions commonly used in spoken Minnan Taiwanese can be considered to be an implication of this educational intention. On the other hand, Barclay's rendition of the same text suggests that it was not his purpose to instruct the readers but rather to convey the biblical text itself to them without adding too much explanation. The conscious avoidance of making it an attentive guide resulted in succinct and somewhat elusive sentences. What then, exactly, was lying behind the nearly directly opposing styles of Moody's and Barclay's translations of *Romans*?

Ideas behind the style: a bibliological approach to the scripture

To understand the background of Moody's educational intention towards Taiwanese readers, it is crucial to see that for all its approachability, what *Lô-má-phoe* deals with is indeed a 'profoundly deep truth, which is very difficult to study and comprehend clearly' ('Cháp-sū' 1908, 111).

As has been previously pointed out, Moody attempts to express the significance of the epistle's verses in a simple tone whilst providing explanations of keywords such as '*Iâ-so Ki-tok ê lô-tsâi* (servant of Jesus Christ),' a concept critical to Christian ideas that might well have been considered new-fangled and difficult to grasp for many of his target readers at the time. Indeed, the topics presented in the discussions section are mostly hardcore theological deliberations, covering the fundamental principles of Christian doctrines from Christology, the recognition of sin, to the idea of justification by faith alone. The choice of highly theological topics as such was Moody's direct response to what he observed as Taiwanese people's selective reception of Christian ideas. Through his daily encounters with Taiwanese audiences during his street preaching, examinations of candidates for baptism and dialogues with native converts, evangelists and ministers, it came to his notice that, in general, Taiwanese people, especially those of Han descent, tended to feel 'foreign or strange, and sometimes, no doubt, confus[ed]' regarding the story of the life and death of Jesus (Moody 1913, 128). Thus, many of the converts themselves tended to be unfamiliar with Christological creeds such as for what purpose Jesus came to this world and in what manner he delivers us. He also saw that by directly interlinking to this unfamiliarity with Jesus, many Taiwanese converts had difficulty understanding concepts such as sin and solifidianism, yet they found it much easier to grasp moral teachings such as those expressed in the Ten Commandments (Moody 1907, 127). Thus, in the discussion section of *Lô-má-phoe*, Moody points out the issue in the following manner (Mûi 1908, 13):

> [W]e often see our brothers and sisters of the church, when they are trying to evangelise heathen peoples, invite them to worship the absolute and true God and not to worship idols, but make no mention to Jesus at all. Sometimes, it is because of their own unfamiliarity [with the topic] that they cannot mention about it; sometimes, it is because of their fear that the heathen people would not understand them; sometimes, it is because they are ashamed, and do not dare mention the crucifixion.

This quote indicates Moody's observation that Taiwanese converts found it difficult to discuss the life and, especially, the death of Jesus to their unconverted neighbours, mostly because of the abstruseness of the concept of Christian salvation itself but also, crucially, because of the sense of shame they felt about the crucifixion of Jesus, which marks not the almighty power but the weakness of the son of god. Importantly, this finding was possibly one of the decisive factors for Moody's choice of *Romans* as the particular text to be translated for Taiwanese readers' use. As is well-known, Paul's theology is quite unique in its seemingly paradoxical message of testifying how what is considered to be foolishness and weakness by 'the wisdom of the world' in fact bears true wisdom and strength. The central theme of *Romans* itself, namely, the justification of the ungodly, is heavily tinged with this mystery as well. For this reason, in the discussion section, Moody consciously canvasses the idea of faith as a surrender to god/Jesus through the recognition of sin by each individual believer, and god's bestowal of salvation as 'un-tián (grace)' (Mûi 1908, 35), an understanding that is largely different from that of many Taiwanese converts', which, far from surrendering, tended to put more emphasis on their own efforts to acquire salvation through the observance of the law such as the Ten Commandments. Thus, Moody reasons that both the attitude of self-regard that has no concern for others ('kò˙ka-tī') and the attitude of self-containment that confides in and relies on one's own capability ('khò ka-tī') are 'the sources of all kinds of evil' (Mûi 1908, 7).

This vigilance against self-justification also closely pertained to the way he criticised Catholicism, which, according to him, is problematic not for 'its worship of Mary and saints and images carved by people' but for its stance that (Mûi 1908, 35):

> Paul is teaching that God, by the Holy Spirit, has breathed righteousness (goodness) into human's hearts, so that people can carry out benefaction (do good); after people have carried out the good deeds, God then justifies that person (regards them as a good soul).

For the idea that people can possess righteousness in their hearts, even though considering it to be something that was originally breathed into them by the Holy Spirit, can easily be led to the acknowledgement of a human ability to take part in their own salvation, which is the direct opposition of the idea of salvation as 'un-tián.' Thus, Moody goes so far as to maintain that the greatest fault of Roman Catholicism is its 'casting away of the grace of God' (Mûi 1908, 35). Critical remarks against Catholicism as such can be seen here and there in the discussion section, which recognisably indicates Moody's self-awareness as a 'Hók-goân-kàu (Reformist)' preacher (Mûi 1908, 35), who aims to make sure that Taiwanese converts can develop a truly Protestant church that is based upon the understanding of salvation, not as an acquired achievement but as 'un-tián,' a gift.

However, it is of critical importance to note that the very basis of Moody's intention to guide Taiwanese Christians comes from his view of the biblical texts, which differed quite a bit from the conventional Protestant ideal of 'sola scriptura,' or, the idea closely pertaining to it that all people, especially the commoners, should be provided the words of god in their own spoken language so that by reading them, they can develop a sound Christian faith by themselves. As has been previously pointed out, Moody's approach to the text of *Romans* was that of modern bibliology, which regards the scripture as a group of historical materials with its own peculiar characteristics and limitations pertaining to the particular time and place in which they were written and compiled. For this reason, in Moody's eyes, it is difficult, if not impossible, for the readers, particularly of the non-Christian world, who themselves are defined by the specific historical context and physical place they belong, to immediately grasp the significance of the biblical text without any guidance. Thus, from his early years as a missionary, Moody argued that '[i]t is a complete misunderstanding of history to suppose that, simply with the Bible in their hands, native Christians would speedily find their way to a developed Protestant Christianity' (Moody 1907, 243). While '[w]e are accustomed in Protestant lands to speak of the Bible as a book for the people,' it is actually a book that even Taiwanese Christians 'find very hard to understand.' If this fact 'astonishes or pains us,' that is (Moody 1912, 238):

> because we have forgotten how much we owe to Church tradition, how dependent we are on modern elucidations and expansions, how terse and how obscure the Scripture often is. We forget how much we read into the words of Scripture, how much we have developed the germs of truth, how busily we have reconciled the contradictions, how much the Spirit has taught us to draw from hints and fragments and flashes of truth.

Thus, Moody points out that the text of the bible, which is often thought of as 'a book for the people' in Protestant lands, is in fact often 'terse' and 'obscure' in itself, and to understand it requires concentrated mental labour to develop 'the germs of truth' from the text and to reconcile the contradicting accounts within it, which cannot be attained without the aid of the cultural and intellectual heritage such as 'Church tradition' and 'modern elucidations and expansions,' as well as the inspiration of 'the Spirit.' Unlike some of the participants of the aforementioned General Conference,

Moody discerned that the simplicity of the style and letters alone could not necessarily help readers truly comprehend the bible's message. Based upon such a view, Moody asserts that 'the heathen are converted not, as a rule, by the Bible, but by the Bible as interpreted by the Church,' and in this sense, 'the Roman Catholic doctrine' that '[t]here is no salvation outside of the Church' is, 'in a far deeper sense than that originally intended,' 'not, at bottom, false' (Moody 1912, 244).

A different perspective can be seen in the Barclay Version bible, which, as mentioned above, is characterised by its intentionally rigid literal translation. Foreseeing the criticism to come, Barclay issued a small pamphlet titled 'Some Thoughts on the New Translation of the Vernacular New Testament' in 1916 at the time of the publication of *Sin-iok*, in which he explained that 'such apparent harshness of rendering is not due to carelessness or incompetence, but to a sincere effort to give with scrupulous accuracy the exact meaning of the inspired writer' (Barclay 1916, 208). This points to the following three aspects of Barclay's attitude towards the biblical text and its readership.

First, Barclay articulates his view that the nature of the scripture is the revelation of god. In the same article, he maintains that if the words of the bible (in this context, the New Testament in particular) are altered as a result of idiomatic and liberal translation, they are no longer and 'cannot be the New Testament of the Christian Church.' Thus, such translations as James Moffatt's *The New Testament: A New Translation* (New York, 1913) and Richard F. Weymouth's *The New Testament in Modern Speech* (London, 1903), both of which were well-known for their bold divergences from the established English renditions, are valuable only as sources for learning 'what distinguished scholars believe to be the meaning of Scripture.' Based upon this belief, Barclay notes that what he and his team had aimed for in their production of the revised POJ New Testament was 'simply to transform the Greek garb of the New Testament into a Chinese garb, leaving the inner meaning so far as might be untouched.' Therefore, 'making an easy translation for the use of women and children' was not their task, nor was it 'to reconcile apparent contradictions, or harmonize discrepancies, or soften harsh expressions, or remove stumbling-blocks.' Their aim, instead, 'was to place the Chinese reader of to-day on the same footing as the Greek reader of the first century' (Barclay 1916, 198). Thus, Barclay maintains that the alteration that happens in the translating process should be limited to the exchange of the garbs, or languages as outer shells encapsulating 'the inner meaning,' which should be left as unscathed and kept in its pure essence as possible, by avoiding any unnecessary interpretations. In other words, Barclay regards the original Greek text as a universal entity, transcendent of the differences of time and space, and believes that whenever it is provided to the readers in their own mother tongue with minimal alteration, whether it be in English or in 'Chinese' or in the Minnan language, every single reader stands 'on the same footing,' the exact equal condition with that of the early converts, the direct receivers of the revelation in its purest form.

Second, closely pertaining to his recognition of the scripture as seen above was his expectation that, with the authentic biblical translation, the contemporary Taiwanese converts would be able to directly receive god's message from the book by themselves, share it among their fellowship and thus autonomously develop their own church community, just as the early converts had done. In Barclay's eyes, it is the autonomous bible-reading, not the guided one, that enables the progress of a strong and independent native church organisation, and, by quoting the words of a Chinese minister 'what we wish is the exact meaning of the original, anything else we can do for ourselves,' he emphasises that the development of an autonomous church based upon an autonomous reading of the bible is exactly what the native church leaders themselves aspire to (Barclay 1916, 199). Barclay further maintains that it is his belief that an idiomatic translation would result in an impairment of the readers' freedom of interpretation; thus he and his team avoided giving any 'decided translation to the exclusion of all others' and aimed 'to provide a text which would be capable of any exegesis, right or wrong, of which the original text was capable' (Barclay 1916, 204). In other words, they attempted to provide as faithful an echo of the original text as possible in order to restage the direct encounter between god's message and its readership, including all the possibilities of 'right or wrong' interpretations coming with it. Based upon such ideas, Barclay expresses his ideal vision that through individual believers' personal encounter with the revelation through the scripture and their 'daily prayerful study of the Word,' 'a living, healthy, growing Church that can never be shaken' may be established (Barclay 1916, 208).

Third, however, it should be noted that Barclay's attention to the absolute universality of the biblical text went hand-in-hand with his relative detachment from the context of Taiwan at the time. By concentrating on the preservation of the form of the biblical text, Barclay, in his translation, consciously chose not to ask or address any questions that would stand in Taiwanese readers' way to understanding the bible's message in the actual socio-cultural situations they found themselves in. This can be clarified through a comparison with Moody's attitude. Not surprisingly, Moody also holds that the biblical text is the revelation of god, stating in *Lô-má-phoe* that the bible is not merely 'a book to instruct people to obey Jesus' teaching' but rather, it is 'the Gospel' itself (Mûi 1908, 39). However, in Moody's eyes, this very same 'Gospel,' which itself is a product of a particular historical context and thus unprecedented for many, could be the most formidable stumbling block for them to understand its message. Thus, in terms of the evangelisation of the Taiwanese people, who had almost no cultural heritage by which to understand the peculiar Judeo-Christian notions, he saw it both practical and necessary for missionaries from the Christian world, such as himself, to guide them by plainly elaborating what he himself was taught and believed to be the correct interpretation of the scripture.

Moody's emphasis on the leadership of foreign missionaries over Taiwanese converts as such closely pertained to his historical view that 'the mind,' or the intellectual sensibility of the contemporary Taiwanese people was, just as that of the early converts used to be, not quite ready to fully grasp the meaning of the Christian message. Regarding that '[t]he History of Dogma' has been 'a history of the human mind,' in which a continuous effort and a gradual obtainment of a deeper understanding of 'the meaning of revelation' has been made, Moody maintains that while it is absolutely wrong to deny Taiwanese converts the title of Christians, it is also a fact that '[t]he least saint in England or in Scotland is greater than the greatest in Formosa because there lie behind us the Dark and Middle Ages, the times of the Reformers, the days of Wesley and Whitefield and Chalmers' (Moody 1907, 141). The bible has been selectively received and partially understood by the people of different ages in their respective context, and among the various dogmas produced by them, some were imperfect and had to be revised. Therefore, the kind of biblical interpretations that were considered to be orthodox in the Protestant Christian community at Moody's time were the fruits of numerous modifications urged by theological challenges such as the Reformations, Methodist movement, and Revivalism, which cannot readily be attained by merely reading the words of the scripture.

To explain this, Moody gives an example from *2 Corinthians*, 'Be ye not unequally yoked together with unbelievers' (6:14), and argues that when 'we,' the contemporaries of the Christian world, read this and 'suppose that Paul was forbidding the marriage of "converted" with "unconverted,"' '[w]e have not, perhaps, so far lost sight of the original sense of the original circumstances.' However, (Moody 1912, 240):

> we scarcely realize how much we have put into Paul's words until we live among native Christians who have no choice but to marry strangers, no chance of ascertaining their spiritual conditions, and are well pleased if they can protect themselves against an idolatrous match.

The realisation that, in Taiwan, Christians were a small minority group, isolated in the dominantly non-Christian society, who struggle daily for 'ascertaining their spiritual conditions' among the scant fellowship and face the difficulty of finding matches of the same faith, made Moody aware, for the first time, of how conventionally he had been granted a certain way to interpret this passage. Thus, although 'it is not easy to recognize,' he observes, 'truths most precious to us are little more than germs and suggestions in Gospels and Epistles' (Moody 1912, 240). For this reason, he maintains that in addition to the text of the bible itself, exegesis to enlarge the mere 'germs and suggestions' in it are essential for the propagation of Christianity, and the most eligible for this task was a missionary from the Christian world, 'an interpreter, an ambassador of Christ, a messenger also of the Church of Christ,' who 'goes laden with the rich inheritance of nineteen Christian centuries' (Moody 1912, 243). Although it was the outcome of Moody's close interest and attempt to respond to the particular context that Taiwanese converts at the time found themselves in, his missiological stance as such was unwittingly at cross-purposes with the idea of native Christians' autonomous evangelism. For this reason, he eventually modified this attitude in the late 1920s, in the face of burgeoning Church autonomy movements among Taiwanese Christians.

Conclusion

As seen by examining Moody's *Lô-má-phoe* and its contrast to the Barclay Version bible, this chapter has clarified how, in the case of biblical translation, the missionary translators' choices of written style could mirror their expectations of the target readers' capability to comprehend the text's message, as well as their perceptions on the biblical text itself. While the two missionary translators were consistent in terms of producing translations for Minnan-speaking readers in POJ, the difference in their writing styles manifested the contrast not only between Moody's guiding attitude and Barclay's permissive stance towards the readers' free interpretations but also between the closely correlated differences in the former's acknowledgement of historical limitations of the scripture and the latter's emphasis on its message's transcendence.

Moody's educational intention towards Taiwanese readers indicated in *Lô-má-phoe* was linked to his missiological idea that missionaries from the Christian world should exercise leadership over their native converts. The foundation of this idea was his view that the biblical text and its words are by no means comprehensible, nor does its message manifest for all, because of their particularity rooted in the Judeo-Christian tradition. It can be pointed out, therefore, that the very reason Moody chose to make *Lô-má-phoe* more than just a translation but also a commentary on *Romans*, the text he presumably considered to be an embodiment of the core Christian ideas, lies here. This was clarified through a comparative examination with Barclay's work. His somewhat detached and non-interference policy, at

A translation designed to guide 101

least through his missionary literature, towards Taiwanese converts resulted in a translation that is as faithful as possible to the original in his eyes, yet precisely because of this attempt, it is a rendition that is difficult to read. Barclay's belief in the universality of the biblical text as the revelation of god, however, persuaded him not to guide but to let Taiwanese converts go on their own journey to form their own notions of the bible's message.

How then, were Moody's and Barclay's missiological standpoints actually received by the Taiwanese readership at the time? And what were the significance and the extent of circulation of Han character bible renditions in Taiwan in comparison to those of POJ scriptures? In order to create a broader picture of the literary works of the English Presbyterian Mission in Taiwan and its relation to the context of the history of Protestant missionary literature, those questions, apart from a fuller comparative analysis between the two missionary translators, will need to be addressed in future studies.

Note

1 For Barclay's *Sin-iok*, the author refers to the text of *New Testament Taiwanese Romanised Han Character Edition.* (2004). Taipei: The Bible Society in Taiwan, which is produced by basing on the Barclay Version, or *Sin Kū Iok ê Sèng-Keng: Tsoân su* [*The New and Old Testament*, in POJ]. (1933). Siōng-hai [Shanghai]: Sèng-Chheh Kong-hōe [British and Foreign Bible Society].

Bibliography

Band, E. (1936) *Barclay of Formosa*. Ginza, Tokyo: Christian Literature Society.
Band, E. (1948) *Working His Purpose Out: The History of the English Presbyterian Mission, 1847–1947*. London: Presbyterian Church of England, Reprint, Taipei: Ch'eng Wen, 1972.
Barclay, T. (1916) Some Thoughts on the New Translation of the Vernacular New Testament. Reprinted in Barclay, T. (2005). *Juzhen-tang Shiliao 8 Ba Keli Zuopin-ji [The Book Room Series 8 collected works of Barclay*, in English and Mandarin Chinese]. Tainan: Taiwan Church News.
Bays, D.H. (2012) *A New History of Christianity in China*. Chichster: Wiley-Blackwell.
Cháp-sū: Chheh-pâng ê Kò-pèh [Miscellaneous: The Book Room's Announcement, in Romanised Minnan Taiwanese (*Pèh-ōe-jī*, hereafter POJ)] (1908) *Tâi-lâm Kàu-hōe-pò [Tainan Church News*, in POJ]. *285 (December): 111*. Included in *Taiwan Jiaohui Gongbao Quanlan: Taiwan Di-yi-fen Baozhi Di 5 Juan (1907-1913) [The Complete Edition of Taiwan Church News: The First Press in Taiwan, Vol. 5 (1907–1913)*, in POJ]. (2004). Tainan: Taiwan Church News.
Douglas, C. (1873) *Chinese-English Dictionary of the Vernacular or Spoken Language of Amoy, with the Principal Variations of the Chang-chew and Chin-chew Dialects*. London: Trübner & Co.

Lai, J. (1988a) Shihua 024 Zaoqi de Minnan-hua Shengjing [Minnan Bibles in Early Years, in Mandarin Chinese]. [Online]. *Lai Yongxiang Zhanglao Shiliao-ku [Elder John Lai's Archives*, in POJ, Mandarin Chinese, Japanese, and English]. Available at: http://www.laijohn.com/BOOK1/024.htm [Accessed: 5 November 2020].

Lai, J. (1988b) Shihua 025 Ma Yage Jianyin Xinyue ji Jiuyue [The New and Old Testament edited by James L. Maxwell, in Mandarin Chinese]. [Online]. Op. cit., *Elder John Lai's Archives*. Available at: http://www.laijohn.com/BOOK1/025.htm [Accessed: 5 November 2020].

Lai, J. (1988c) Shihua 032 Xiamen-yin Xin-zidian [The New Amoy Dictionary, in Mandarin Chinese]. [Online]. Op. cit., *Elder John Lai's Archives*. Available at: http://www.laijohn.com/1/032.htm [Accessed: 3 November 2020].

Lîm, C. (2013) Lâng-lâng Ài-thák ê *Choân-bîn Tâi-gú Shèng-keng* [*Common Taiwanese Bible* as Everyone's Favourite, in POJ with Han characters]. *Xin-Shizhe Zazhi [The New Messenger*, in POJ, POJ with Han characters, and Mandarin Chinese]. 137 (August): 74–75. [Online]. Op. cit., *Elder John Lai's Archives*. Available at: http://www.laijohn.com/Bible/F5/introd/Lim,Ciok/2013.08.htm [Accessed: 7 November 2020].

Lin, H. (2017) Yi-jing yu Yuyan-xue: Ba Keli Taiyu *Shengjing* de Yufa Wenti [Bible Translation and Linguistics: The Issue of Grammar in Barclay's Taiwanese Bible, in Mandarin Chinese]. *Taiwan Wenxue Yanjiu Jikan [Studies in Taiwan Literature*, in Mandarin Chinese] 20 (February): 1–24.

Maxwell, J.L. (1871) Foreign Missions: Letters from China. *The Messenger & Missionary Record of the Presbyterian Church in England* 4(12): 274–277.

Missionary paragraphs: Dr. Barclay's New Task. (1925) *The Presbyterian Messenger*. 965 (August): 95.

Moody, C.N. (1907) *The Heathen Heart: An Account of the Reception of the Gospel Among the Chinese of Formosa*. Edinburgh: Oliphant, Anderson & Ferrier.

Moody, C.N. (1912). *The Satins of Formosa: Life and Worship in a Chinese Church*. Edinburgh: Oliphant, Anderson & Ferrier.

Moody, C.N. (1913) The Western Form of Christianity. *The East & the West: A Quarterly Review for the Study of Missions* 11: 121–146.

Moody, C.N. (1932) *The King's Guests: A Strange Formosan Fellowship*. London: H. R. Allenson.

Moody, P.C. (n.d.) *Campbell Moody: Missionary and Scholar*, as Âng, Pek-kî. (2005). *Juzhen-tang Shiliao 4 Xuanjiao-Xuezhe Mei Jianwu [The Book Room Series 4 Campbell Moody: Missionary and Scholar*, in English and Mandarin Chinese]. Tainan: Taiwan Church News.

Mûi, K. (1908) *Lô-má-phoe I kàu VIII chiu^n Sin Hoan-èk ê Pèk-bûn í-kìp Chù-kái, Kóe-seh, Káng [New Vernacular Translation of and Commentary on Romans I-VIII*, in POJ]. Tâi-lâm [Tainan]: Chū-tin-tông [the Book Room]. Reprinted in Moody, Campbell N. (2006). *Juzhen-tang Shiliao 5 Mei Jianwu Zuopin-ji [The Book Room Series 5 Collected Works of Campbell Moody*, in POJ and Mandarin Chinese]. Tainan: Taiwan Church News.

Murakami, Y. (1968) Hakuwazi no Hensen to Minnan-go yaku Seisyo: Purotesutanto Bunsyo Dendou ni tsuite no Oboe-gaki [Transition of POJ and Minnan-translated

Bible: A Note on Protestant Literary Evangelism, in Japanese]. *Yamato Bunka* [*Yamato Culture*, in Japanese] 48 (March): 96–118.
Barclay, T. (1916) *Sin-iok [The New Testament] as New Testament Taiwanese Romanised Han Character Edition*. (2004) Taipei: The Bible Society in Taiwan.
Yates, M.T., Nelson, R., and Barrett, E.R. (eds.) (1878) *Records of the General Conference of the Protestant Missionaries of China, held at Shanghai, May 10–24, 1877*. (1878) Shanghai: Presbyterian Mission Press, Reprint, Taipei: Ch'eng Wen, 1973.
Tân, B. (2015) Baihua-zi de Qiyuan yu zai Taiwan de Fazhan [The Origins of Pe̍h-ōe-jī and its Development in Taiwan, in Mandarin Chinese]. Ph.D. Dissertation. National Taiwan Normal University. Available at: http://etds.lib.ntnu.edu.tw/cgi-bin/gs32/gsweb.cgi/ccd=XFk77f/record?r1=1&h1=0#XXXX [Accessed: 5 November 2020].
The Bible Society in Taiwan. (2006) Baihua-zi Shengjing de Youlai [The Origin of POJ Bible, in Mandarin Chinese]. Posted as 'Xiamen Luoma-zi Shengjing de Youlai [The Origin of Bibles in the Romanised Amoy, in Mandarin Chinese]. [Online]. Op. cit., *Elder John Lai's Archives*. Available at: http://www.laijohn.com/Bible/F/about/skkh.htm [Accessed: 5 November 2020].
Kee, H.C. (1993) *The Cambridge Annotated Study Bible: New Revised Standard Version*. Cambridge: Cambridge University Press.
The American Bible Society. (1902) *The Holy Scriptures of the Old and New Testament in the Chinese Literary Language, Plain Style*. Translated by S. I. J. Schereschewsky. Yokohama: Fukuin Printing Company. [Online]. Available at: https://archive.org/details/holyscripturesof00sche [Accessed: 7 November 2020].
Tiedemann, R.G. (ed.) (2010) *Handbook of Christianity in China*, vol. 2, 1800 to Present. Leiden: Brill.
Xili 1876 nian Tainan Shenxue-xiao (Daxue) Kaishe yihou zhi Xuesheng Xingming [AD 1876 Roll of Former and Current Students since the Establishment of Tainan Theological College (the College), in Mandarin Chinese]. (1957) *Sîn-ha̍k kap Kàu-hōe: Qingzhu Bashi-zhounian Te-kan hao [Theology and Church: The Eightieth Anniversary Special Issue,* in POJ and Mandarin Chinese]. Tainan: Tainan Theological College and Seminary.
Xinyue Quanshu [the New Testament, in Mandarin Chinese]. (1857) Translated by W. H. Medhurst and J. Stronach. Shanghai: Mohai Shuguan. [Online]. Available at: https://bible.fhl.net/ob/nob.html?book=90 [Accessed: 7 November 2020].
Zhang, M. (2005) *Kaiqi Xinyan: 'Taiwan-fucheng Jiaohui-bao' yu Zhanglao Jiaohui de Jidu-tu Jiaoyu [Opening the Eyes of Minds: 'Taiwan Capital Church News' and Christian Education in Presbyterian Church,* in Mandarin Chinese]. Tainan: Renguang Publishing Company.

Index

Note: Page numbers in *italics* indicate figures, **bold** indicate tables, and page numbers with "n" indicates the end notes in the text.

accommodation ix, 2, 3, 14, 15;
 Christian teachings 1, 13; Jesuit
 policy of ix; policy 2, 3, 14
accomodatio 1
Acts of the Apostles (Stronach) 34, 84
Acu-dŏ, translation of *28*
acu no michi see path of evil
Aid to the eyes and ears of Western
 scholars *see Xiru ermu zi*
Aleni, Giulio x, 7, 10, 19n16, 20n34
Amen 15, 20n35
anima (soul) 9, 15, 16
Anjirō 48, 49
Appenzeller, H.G. 58
argumentative reasoning (*ratiocinatio*) x
Aristotle 3, 41, 43, 44
Artes see grammar
Arundell, Thomas 74–75
Auguſt(us) 33
Ave 15

Bacon, Francis 4
badele see Pater
Barclay, Thomas xii, xiii, 82, 85, 93,
 97, 98
Barclay Version bible 97
Bartoli, Daniello 5
Bianchi, Alessandro ix, x, xiii, 52n5
Bible: Barclay Version 97; books of
 33; primacy of xi; translation into
 Japanese language xi; translations in
 Korean language 57–58, 79; *see also*
 Chinese, Bible; Korean Bible

biblical exegesis 32
bibliographic aspects of *Sanctos* 31
Biblioteca Marciana 52n3
biwa hōshi 50
Board of Revisers in Korea 63
Board of Translators of New
 Testament *62*
board translations of Korean Bible 62–63
Bodleian Library copy of *Sanctos*
 25, 52n3
Book of Ruth see Lō-tek ê Chheh
Book Room 81, 85
Brancati, Francesco x, 2, 11–15, 17,
 20n29
British and Foreign Bible Society
 61–62, 85, 101n1
Brockey, Liam 6, 18n4
Buddhism 69; Buddhist monk 11;
 history of translation of viii;
 influence of 11
buhwal see resurrection
Bunyan, John 67
Burke, Peter xiv

Caminho da maldade see path of evil
Campbell, William 82
Cardinal Dom Henrique of Portugal 41
Cartilha see Christian Doctrine
catechisms 2, 11, 15, 17, 20n28, 49;
 comparative examination 11–12; for
 Portuguese children 12
Cathalagus Sanctorum 35, 53n12
Catholicism 95

106 Index

Celiang fayi 6
Chang-jik, Yi *62*
Changjik, Yi xiii
Cheung, Martha 17n1
China/Chinese: Bible translation into Korean Bible 60, 61; Christianity in viii; decision to adopt Buddhist terminology x; history of translation and interpreting in 1–2; impact on Jesuit missions in xi; language in eyes of Western missionaries 3–7; missionaries in xiii, 2–3; missionary literature in 81, 83–85; philosophical tradition 6; production of Christian literature in 81; readership 9; textual transmission in 8; traditional historiography 1; value of written language in 4
Chinese-English Dictionary of the Vernacular or Spoken Language of Amoy (Douglas) 84
Chinese–Portuguese dictionary 6; *see also Dicionário Português-Chinês*
Christian Doctrine 12, 14, 32; apology of 7, 18n13; dissemination in late-imperial China 2; fundamental principles from Christology 94
On the Christian Expedition in China *see De Christiana Expeditione apud Sinas*
Christianity 12; in China viii; pillars of 19n14; ritual and liturgic aspects in plain language 12; spreading throughout Korea 58; in Taiwan 99–100
Christian literature x, 81
chuanyu see word-transmitters
Chung-sam, Kim *62*
Church News 81, 86
Clark, Allen 78
classical Chinese xi, 58, 64
Cloud Dream of the Nine, The (Manjung) 67
Coelho, Gasper 49
commandment 9
communication viii, 83; verbal 4
compassion xii, 72
compendium of the lives of the saints *see Sanctos no gosagueo no uchi nuqigaqi*

Compendium on the Christian doctrine *see Tianzhu jiaoyao*
Confucian canon 7, 17
Confucian ethical system 7
Confucian philosophy xi
Confucian terminology in missionary publications 11
Confucius 8
Constitutiones Societatis Iesu (de Loyola) 3
Constitutions of Oxford (Arundell) 74
Constitutions of the Society of Jesus *see Constitutiones Societatis Iesu*
'construed orally' (*kou yi*) 8
controversial translation of Korean Bible 73–75; faithfulness *vs.* naturalization 75–77; linguistic differences 77–79
Council of Trent x–xi
Counter-Reformation Europe 41, 52
cultural translation: of China, Korea and Japan xiv; for Japanese readership 43–48; *Sanctos* as example of 24, 40–41
Cuonhoa see forensic language

da Cruz, Gaspar 4, 18n9
Dainichi see God
Dainichi nyorai (Supreme Buddha of Cosmos) x
da Rocha, João x, 2, 11, 13–14, 16
da Varazze, Jacopo 35
Decemb(er) 33
De Christiana Expeditione apud Sinas (Ricci) 4
de Granada, Luis 24, 25, 34–35, 41–43, 46, 50–52; portrait of *42*; survey of *kirishitanban* literature 34
Delegates' Version: in classical Chinese 93; into POJ 84–85; in *Wen-li* 81
D'Elia, Pasquale 9
Dell'Istoria della Compagnia de Gesu: La Cina (Bartoli) 5
de Loyola, Ignatius 3
de Mendoza, Gonzáles 4
de Mesquita, Diogo, ix, 51
de Poirot, Louis Antone 17
devotio moderna movement in Europe x
Dias Jr., Manuel 7

Dicionário see Dicionário
    Português-Chinês
Dicionário Português-Chinês 6, 9, 10;
    semantic interpretations in 11
Dictionary of the Amoy Vernacular
    Spoken Throughout the Prefectures
    of Chin-chiu, Chiang-chiu, and
    Formosa, A (Campbell) 82
Dictionnaire Coréen-Français 61
Diogo, Hibiya Ryōkei 49
dissemination: of Christian doctrine
    2; of European knowledge 2; of
    Western knowledge 12
divination 14
Doctrina Christaã see Christian Doctrine
doctrinal gathering/assembly 16;
    see also ecclesia
Dominicans 2, 41
Doty, Elihu 84
Douglas, Carstairs 84
Dutch Reformed Church in America
    (DRCA) 84
duyu see word-measurers

ecclesia 9, 15, 16, 33; primitiva ix
educational monopoly xii
On the education of children 14–15
Egelexiya (church) 9
e'lajiya see Gratia
Elements of geometry see Jihe yuanben
emoni (mother) 72
Emperador 33
En-mun 70
Euclid's Elements, Books I-VI xiii
Eusebius Cesariense 35
Evangelicae Historiae Imagines
    (Nadal) x, 20n34
evil practices 14
evil spirits 14
Explanations on the Incarnation of
    the Lord of Heaven see Tianzhu
    jiansheng chuxiang jingjie
Extracts from the Acts of the Saints
    see Sanctos no gosagueo no uchi
    nuqigaqi

fadu see law/moral standard
faithfulness 75–77
Falato, Giulia viii, x
Father Balthasar Gago 49

Father Melchior Nunes 49
fei 10
feilüe see Filius
feiluosuofeiya 10
feilusuofeiya 10
fengshui see making offerings
Fernandes, João 49
Filius 15
Flos Sanctorum 35, 53n12
forensic language 5
'fortitude', virtue of 44, 45
Four Books and Five Classics 7
Franciscans 2
Fróis, Luis 49, 50
Fukushima, K. 35, 37, 53n7
Fundación Universitaria Española 52n4
Furtado, Francisco 19n15
Fu Xi see Three Sovereigns

Gale, James Scarth xii, 57, 59,
    62, 66–68, 70–72; criticisms on
    translation 77; friendship with Yi
    59–60; naturalising approach 76, 78;
    translation of Korean Bible 73, 75
General Conference of Protestant
    missionaries in China 83
Genesis 34
Genette, G.R. 39
gewu qiongli 10
Gibson, Harriet E. 67
Gô Béng 89
Gô Bíkiàn 90
God x, 32, 48, 57, 60–61, 71, 74, 78;
    in Chinese xii; power on Earth 14;
    word of 81
Gospel According to Luke see Lō-ka
    Hok-im Toàn
Gospel According to Mark see Má-kó
    Hok-im Toàn
Gospel of John 61
Gospel of Luke 60, 61
Gospel of Mark xi
Gougu yi 6
Grammaire Coreenne 61
grammar 12, 31, 67; Korean 65, 66;
    vernacular 57
Gratia 15
Guangqi, Xu xiii, 6, 18n13, 19n14,
    20n32
guanhua 4, 9, 10, 18n10

108 Index

Guia de pecadores 51
gukmun see national script
Gutenberg printing press, ix
gyeongbae 72

hagiographies in *Sanctos* 34–35
Hȧk-kiong, Lîm 90
hananim see God
Han characters: bible renditions 92–93, 101; biblical translations 90; literature in Mandarin in 83, 85; *Wen-li* literature in 83, 85
Hangeul xii, 57, 63–65, 67–70, 79
Hanja xii, 64, 68–70, 79
hanmun xi, 68
heart/mind 9, 11
Heike monogatari 46, 50
heraldic symbolism 46
Hiàn-chiong, Ṅg 90
Historia Ecclesiatica (Eusebius) 35
On the History of the Society of Jesus: China see *Dell'Istoria della Compagnia de Gesu: La Cina*
Hōin, Vicente xiii
Hȯk-goânkàu (Reformist) 95
Holy Scriptures of the Old and New Testament in the Chinese Literary Language, Plain Style, The (Schereschewsky) 92
Holy Trinity 15
Hongjun, Baek 58
horizontal writing 29
Hsia, Ronnie Po-chia xiv 19n17
Hsiang-Wei, Lin 93
hun see soul
Hung, Eva 17n1

Iâ-so.̇ ê lô-tsâi 87
Iâ-so Ki-tok ê lô-tsâi (servant of Jesus Christ) 87, 88, 94
Illustrated explanations of the Incarnation of the Lord of Heaven (Aleni) x, 20n34
Illustrations of Gospel Stories see *Evangelicae historiae imagines*
individual translations of Korean Bible 59–60, 62, 63
interdenominational cooperation 81
interlingual equivalents x
interlingual translation *28*, 40

interpreters 8, 100
intersemiotic translation x, 40
intertextuality of *Sanctos* translation 33–40
Introduction del symbolo de la fe (de Granada) 24, 34–35, 41, 43, 52n18; comparison with *Sanctos* 38–39, 44; translation of 35, 48–50
Introduction to the Symbol of the Faith see *Introduction del symbolo de la fe*
Iok Han Thoan Hok Im Su (Gospel According to John) (Doty) 84
iter studiorum 7
Iú-sêng, Tân 90

jabi see compassion
Jade Pass 18n2
Jaepil, Seo 65
Jakobson, Roman 40
Japan: impact on Jesuit missions in xi; missionaries in xiii
Japanese Jesuits xiii, 51; brothers 49, 51
Japanese-language: Christian devotional literature 24; *Sanctos* in 31–32; text 29, 31
Jesuit(s) 1–2, 24; in Beijing xi; in China 6; French 61; library in Japan 41; literary endeavours 7; mission in Chinese territory 3–4; policy of accommodation ix; printed translation of New Testament in Kyoto xi; publishing *Introduction del symbolo de la fe* 53n18; system of transliteration 29; translation project 19n15
Jesuit missionaries ix; in Japan 35; prolific activities of 53n6
Jesuit Mission Press 24, 25
Jesuit translation practices in Japan x, 25; content, intertextuality and concept of translation 33–40; cultural translation for Japanese readership 43–48; material studies and textual analysis 25–27; *Sanctos* as example of cultural translation 40; seminal research on *Sanctos* 24–25
ji see sign
jiaohui see doctrinal gathering/ assembly; *ecclesia*
Jiaoyao jielüe 13

Jiaoyou lun 17
jie 9
Jihe yuanben xiii, 6, 8
Jinki, Kim 58
John, Griffith 85
John 2:4, comparison of Korean translations of 72, *72*
John of Damascus 34
Jolliffe, Pia ix, x, xiii, 24, 53n17
Jorge, Marcos 12
Joseon keulja 65, 66
Joseon Korea 61
Joseon-mal xii, 59, 63–65, 79
Judeo-Christian: notions 99; tradition 100
Junggeun, Kim 67

kana 29, 32, 53n8
kanbun kundoku 28
Kangxi emperor 2, 11
kanji 29, 53n8
Keller, Hellen 89
Kiaer, Jieun xii
Kilgour 76, 77
Kiljun, Yu 69
King Kojong 64
King Sejong the Great xi, 69
kirishitan 51, 53n10
kirishitanban 25, 29, 31, 32, 51; Roman type transcriptions in 32; translations 43
*koin*é 4
Korea 58; American Presbyterian missionary arrival xi; Bible translations in 79; Christian community formation in xi; missionaries in xiii; modernization 66
Korean Bible 57; Bible translators and missionary grammarians 57–59; board of revisers and official translation 61; collaboration between western missionaries and Korean *josa* 59–60; controversial translation 73–79; history of Bible translation 63; James Gale's Bible 67; making of 64; pragmatic translation 68–71; problems of *Joseon Mal-ro* 'into the Korean vernacular', 63–65; Ross and team 60–61; timeline of Bible translations 61–63; translating key terms 71–73
Korean-English Dictionary, A 67
Korean-English dictionary 65
Korean *josa* 59–61
Korean language 57, 61, 77
Korean Protestant Christianity xii
Korean vernacular 79; problems of *Joseon Mal-ro* 'into 63–65
Korean *yangban* literati xi
Kū-iok ê Sèng-keng (The Old Testament) (Barclay) 85
Kü-iok ê Sin-keng (The Old Testament) (Maxwell) 85
kuk ('country') 69
Kukhanmun 68, 69

Lán ê Kiù-chú Iâ-so Ki-tok ê Sin-iok (Maxwell) 84
language learning 3; analysis of written and spoken varieties of language 5–6; collaborative aspects of formative and missionary activities 6; cultured dialogue between interlocutors 6–7; verbal communication and dictation 4–5; written language value in China 4
Laozi 8
La più equivoca lingua e lettera che si ritruovi see Chinese, language in eyes of Western missionaries
law/moral standard 9
Legenda Aurea see Flos Sanctorum
Lessons for the Congregation of Angels (Brancati) x, 2, 11–12, 13, 15, 16, 17, 19n25, 20n29
Libro de la oracion y meditacion 51
ling see soul
línguas estranhas 3
On Linguistic Aspects of Translation (Jakobson) 40
linguistic differences in Korean Bible 77–79
linguistic negotiation 8
literati xiii, 2, 10, 11, 74, 83; Chinese 10; Korean xi; late Ming 7; yangban 67
litui zhi fa 11
lixue 10
logographic nature of Chinese characters 4

Lō-ka Hok-im Toān (Talmage) 84
Lok-tia, Lu 85
Lô-má-phoe (Moody) 82–83, 86;
   bibliological approach to scripture
   94–100; designed for clarity and
   approachability 86–90; Romans
   translated text comparison with
   Barclay's *Sin-iok* 91; translation
   designed to guide 90–93
Lô-má-phoe I kàu VIII chiu^n Sin Hoan-ėk ê Pėk-bûn í-kip Tsùkái, Kóe-seh, Káng see Lô-má-phoë
London Missionary Society (LMS) 84
Longobardo, Niccolò 7
López-Gay, J. 50, 53n12
Lō-tek ê Chheh (Talmage) 84
Loureiro, R.M. 35
lùt-hoat ê kui-lē 92

Macintyre, John 58, 60
Ma-hui, Ng 85
making offerings 14
Makita, Tominaga 29
Má-kó Hok-im Toān (Talmage) 84
Mandamento see commandment
Mandarin xiii, 4, 19n22; literature 84;
   New Testament in 92; vernacular 81, 83
Manjung, Kim 67
Manuel Dias the Elder 6
Mark 12:18, 73
Martinho, Hara xiii, 51
Masini, Federico 19n20
Maxwell, James L. 84
Mayor, Thomas 53n18
Medhurst, Walter H. 84, 92
mercy xii
Method and System of the Studies of
   the Society of Jesus *see Ratio atque Institutio Studiorum Societatis Iesu*
Methodist movement 99
methods and principles of measurement
   see Celiang fayi
Miller, Hugh 74–76, 78
Mingjian x
Minnan 84, 85
Minnan Taiwanese xii–xiii, 81, 89;
   bible translation 86; phrasing 92;
   vernacular text of *Lô-má-phoe* 90–92
Mino, Kazue xiii

missionaries: Catholic xiii–xiv; in
   China 2; European 6–7; grammarians
   65–67; in Japan xiii; in Korea xiii;
   LMS missionaries role in writing
   system 84; Protestant xiii–xiv
   82; translators 75; *see also* Jesuit
   missionaries
missionary literature: in China 81,
   83–85; in Greater China 81, 83–85;
   in Taiwan 83–85
modus operandi of Chinese
   translators 8
modus traducendi of Chinese
   translators 8
Moffatt, James 97
Monica, Hibiya xiii, 49–50
Moody, Campbell N. xii, xiii, 82, 86,
   88, 90–101
Moretti, Laura 52n5
morphemes 10
morte (death) 33
multi-linguality 82
Mungello, D.E. 18n4
Myong-jun, Kim 62

Nadal, Jerónimo x, 20n34
Nanjing Incident (1616) 9–10, 12,
   18n5, 18n13
National Bible Society of Scotland *see*
   Scottish Bible Society
national script xii, 64
naturalization 75–77
negotiations viii, 1, 7; doctrinal 14, 17;
   linguistic x, 8, 14, 17; role of local
   literati in 2
Neo-Confucianism 10, 72
Nevius, John Livingstone xi–xii, 59
Nevius Method 59, 63
*New Testament, The: A New
   Translation* (Moffatt) 97
New Testament, The of Taiwan *see Sin-iok* (Barclay)
New Testament in Modern Speech, The
   (Weymouth) 97
*New Vernacular Translation of and
   Commentary on Romans I-VIII*
   (Moody) xii, 82
Nijugocagio 49
non-Han cultures 1
nukigaki 37

Opium Wars (1839–1842/1856–1860) 1
Opuscula Divi Thomae 41
Ostrom, Alvin 84
Our Lord Jesus Christ's New Testament
  see *Lán ê Kiù-chú Iâ-so Ki-tok ê*
  Sin-iok
Outline of the essential teachings (of
  Christian doctrine) 13
Outline of the Western learning (Aleni)
  7, 10

Pacheco, Diego 51
padre 9
page layout of *Sanctos* 27–33
Passion and Death of our Saviour 47
Pater 15
path of evil 28
Paulo, Yōhō Ken xiii, 49
Paul of Tarsus ix
Paz, Octavio viii
Pėh-ōe-jī (POJ) xii, 81, 90; completion
  of translation of biblical texts 85;
  LMS missionaries role in writing
  system 84; *Lô-má-phoe* in 86; *New*
  Testament (Barclay) 82, 85, 97; *Old*
  Testament (Barclay) 82; syllables 89;
  translation of *Romans* 90
philosophia 10
phonemic loans 2–3, 9–11, 14–15, 17
Pilgrim's Progress, The (Bunyan) 67
Pôe-eng, Ong 90
Portuguese Padroado (Assistancy) in
  Asia 2
pragmatic translation of Korean Bible
  68–71
prayers 12
Presbyterian Church of England (PCE)
  81, 84
Presiding Translator 8
Primer of the Holy Christian doctrine
  (da Rocha) x, 2, 11–12, 13, 15,
  16, 17
primitive Church *see ecclesia, primitiva*
Principles of *Gougu see Gougu yi*
Protestants 2; Christianity xii, 96;
  missionaries 82
Punyuk ta toyusso 62

Qian, Zhi 8
Qianzi wen 6

Index 111

Qing Empire 81–84
qiongli xue 10–11
Que, Shen 18n13

Rakuyōshū dictionary 53n8
Ratio atque Institutio Studiorum
  Societatis Iesu 3
Ratio studiorum, ix, 18n7
readership: Brancati 13; Catholic and
  Protestant 41; Chinese 9; da Rocha
  12; Japanese 43–48; Taiwanese 101
Reformations xi, 99
relazioni 4
resurrection 13, 73
Revised Re-Officialised Translation 63
Revivalism 99
Reynolds, W.D. 58–59, 61, *62*, 77
Rho, Giacomo 19n15
Ricci, Matteo viii–ix, xi, xiii, 3–4, 6,
  9, 16
Rites Controversy 2, 17, 18n5
Roman Catholic doctrine 97
Romanised Minnan bible renditions 84
Romanised text of *Sanctos* 29
Romans 86–88; decisive factors for
  Moody's choice of 95; Moody's
  translation of xiii, 93, 96; *Romans*
  2:7, 90; *Romans* 2:26, 92; *Romans*
  8:24, 93
Ross, John xi, xii, 58, 66, 72; Bible
  translation 59; translation of Luke's
  Gospel 60
Ruggieri, Michele viii–ix, x, 3, 6, 11,
  14, 16
Rules for reciting the rosary (da
  Rocha) 16

sacerdote 9
sacraments 13, 15, 16, 20n37
sacramentum 15, 16
Sacred Scriptures: brief record of 13;
  vernacular translations of xi
sagelamengduo see sacramentum
Saint Agatha 43
Saint Barbara 44, 46–47
Saint Christopher 40
Saint Clara 47
Saint Eulalia 43–44, 47
Saint Ignatius of Loyola 46
Saint John the Apostle 40

Index

Saint John the Baptist 40
Saint Laurence 43
Saint Paul the Apostle 40
Saint Peter 40
Saint Thomas of Aquinas 43
Saint Vincent 43
Sakwajinam 67
Salve 15, 20n35
Sanctos no gosagueo no uchi nuqigaqi ix, 24, 52, 53n10; Bodleian Library copy 25; comparison between book structure, pagination and text arrangement *30*; comparison between two historiated initials in *26*, *30*; conspectus of content and textual sources 36–37; content, intertextuality and concept of translation 33–40; cultural translation for Japanese readership 43–48; as example of cultural translation 40–41; first page of bilingual glossary *28*; frontispiece of *27*; materiality of language 27–33; material studies and textual analysis 25–28; seminal research on 24–25; Spanish text comparison with Japanese version 35, 38–39, 43, 46; translators and translation processes 48–51
Sang-ryun, Seo 58
San Kurara see Saint Clara
San Orara see Saint Eulalia
Satow, E.M. 37
saze'erduode (priest) 9
Schereschewsky, S.I.J. 85, 92
Schreck, Johann Terrenz 19n15
Scottish Bible Society 61
Scranton, W.B. 58
Segunda parte de la Introduction del symbolo de la fe (Luis de Granada) 25, 40, *45*
semantic loans 10
Semedo, Alvaro 5, 18n13
seng see Buddhism, Buddhist monk
seong 72
Seongha, Yi 58–60
Seongjun, Yu 69
Seonhan-mun 69
shen'erfu see Salve
Shengjing yuelu 13, 15
sheren see tongue–men

shijie see Ten Commandments
sibiliduo sanduo see Spiritus Sanctus
sign 16
Si-gyeong, Ju 71
sin 72
Sin-iok (Barclay) 85, 97, 101n1; Romans translated text comparison with Moody's *Lô-má-phoe* 91
Sino-Western relations 2
Siōng-tè ê hok-im 87
Sishu wujing see Four Books and Five Classics
siū-tiàu ê sù-tô, 87
sola scriptura xi, 96
Soltau, Stanley 78
Songnian zhugui cheng. Rules for reciting the rosary
Sorae Church 58
Sorae Kyohoe see Sorae Church
soul 9, 16
Spanish spirituality 43
speaking well (*bene parlare*) 4–5
Spiritus Sanctus 15
Standaert, Nicolas 18n4, 19n17
St. Ignatius's Society of Jesus 3
St. Mark's Gospel in Korean 58
Stove god 14
Stronach, John 84, 92
suanming see divination
Sujeong, Yi 58
Summa Contra Gentiles 41
Summa Theologica (Thomas) 41
Sú-tô Hêngtoãn see Acts of the Apostles
Symeon the Metaphrast 34, 37

Tai-oan-Hu-sia[n] Kau-hōe-po see Church News
Taiwan: Christianity in 99–100; missionary literature in 83–85; with Presbyterian Church of England xii–xiii; Taiwanese readership 101; *see also* Minnan Taiwanese
Taiwan Capital Church News see Church News
Talmage, John V.N. 84
Tasan see Yakyong, Jeong
tategaki see vertical writing
Ten Commandments 13–14, 94, 95
Tenshō Embassy 24, 50–51, 52n4
text reduction methods 37

theological roots 72
Thousand Character Classic *see Qianzi wen*
Thousand Character Series, The (Gale) 68
Three Sovereigns 5
Tianshen hui ke see Lessons for the Congregation of Angels
Tianzhuguo sen x
Tianzhu jiansheng chuxiang jingjie see Illustrated explanations of the Incarnation of the Lord of Heaven
Tianzhu jiaoyao (Ricci) 9
Tianzhu shengjiao qimeng see Primer of the Holy Christian doctrine
Tianzhu shilü see True Record of the Lord of Heaven, The
Tianzhu shiyi see True Meaning of the Lord of Heaven, The
timeline of Korean Bible translations 61–62; board translations 62–63; individual translations 62
Tingyun, Yang 7, 19n14
Tinos, Ellis 52n5
Tiyeonroyeokjeong 67
tongue–men 1
Tongyou jiaoyu see On the education of children
tongzi see readership
Tō-sam, Tiun 90
translation viii, xiii, 2, 37; of *Acudŏ 28*; board translations of Korean Bible 62–63; concept of *Sanctos* 33–40; controversial *see* controversial translation of Korean Bible; cultural *see* cultural translation; history of Buddhism viii; interlingual *28*, 40; intersemiotic x, 40; key terms and case study 11–16; practices 40; pragmatic *see* pragmatic translation of Korean Bible; processes 7–11, 48–51; of Sacred Scriptures xi; word-for-word translations 40
translators 48–51
Tratado das coisas da China see Treatise on China
Treatise on China (da Cruz) 18n9
Tridentine doctrine 43
Trigault, Nicolas 4, 7

Index 113

True Meaning of the Lord of Heaven, The (Ricci) xi, 12
True Record of the Lord of Heaven, The (Ruggieri) x, 11, 12. 14
Tsok-pang, Ng 90
Twenty-Four Paragons of Filial Piety, The 89
2 Corinthians 99
two-fold analysis 10
typography of *Sanctos* 27–33

Underwood, Revs. H.G. 58, *62*, 66
Ungchan, Yi 58, 59
Union Version in Mandarin vernacular 81
Un-jin, Lim 85
un-tián 95
untranslated foreign words in *Sanctos* 33

Vagnone, Alfonso 10, 14, 16
Valignano, Alessandro ix, 3, 18n8, 53n8
verbal communication and dictation 4
vertical writing 29
Vieira, António 3
Vincente, Hōin 49
Vitae Sanctorum Patrum 34
von Bell, Johann Adam Schall 19n15

wahon 27, 29, 31
Ward, H.N. 49, 50
wen-li xiii; Delegates' Version in 81; literature 83; Old Testament texts 84–85; renditions in Han characters 85
Western learning (Vagnone) 1, 7, 10–11, 17
Weymouth, Richard F. 97
word-for-word translations 40
word-measurers 8
word-transmitters 8
writing well (*bene scrivere*) 4
written language value in China 4

Xavier, Francis viii, x, 48–49
xi 33
xian Zao see Stove god
xiefa see evil practices
xieshen see evil spirits
xingxue 10
xin see heart/mind

Xiru ermu zi (Trigault) 9
Xiugai lifa qing fang yong Tang Ruowang Luo Yagu shu. 18n12
Xixue see Western learning
xixue dongjian see Western learning
Xixue fan see Outline of the Western learning
Xiyu 18n2

Yakyong, Jeong xi
yameng see Amen

yanima see anima
yawu see Ave
yokogaki see horizontal writing
Yoshimi, Orii 48
Yumen guan *see* Jade Pass
Yumongcheonja see Thousand Character Series, The

Zhizao, Li xiii, 19n14
Zhuangzi 8
zhu yi see Presiding Translator

For Product Safety Concerns and Information please contact our EU representative GPSR@taylorandfrancis.com
Taylor & Francis Verlag GmbH, Kaufingerstraße 24, 80331 München, Germany

www.ingramcontent.com/pod-product-compliance
Lightning Source LLC
Chambersburg PA
CBHW051753230426
43670CB00012B/2274